LOST

BRITISH FORTS

of

LONG ISLAND

DAVID M. GRIFFIN

THE
History
PRESS

Published by The History Press
Charleston, SC
www.historypress.net

Front cover, bottom: *Halt at the Outpost*, painting by Alfred Wordsworth Thompson, 1881.
Public domain.
Back Cover, bottom: "View of the neck & lines at Boston with the rebel works at Roxburgh.
14th Febry 1776." *From* Archibald Robertson: His Diaries and Sketches in America, 1762–
1780, *New York Public Library Digital Collections.*

First published 2017

Manufactured in the United States

ISBN 9781625858535

Library of Congress Control Number: 2017941352

Notice: The information in this book is true and complete to the best of our knowledge. It is
offered without guarantee on the part of the author or The History Press. The author and
The History Press disclaim all liability in connection with the use of this book.

To my son Avery, who has accompanied me on many a quest.

CONTENTS

Acknowledgements

There are many people I wish to thank for their great insight and assistance during my many months of research and writing. It has truly been an educational and inspiring time for me, and I have greatly expanded my comprehension of early Long Island history by sharing research with other colleagues, local historians and research librarians across the region. I am also grateful to all the historical societies of Long Island and the local history libraries, many of which helped me in my research. All combined, these institutions knit together our rich regional history and preserve our many historical sites and documents for future generations.

I would like to personally thank the Society for the Preservation of Long Island Antiquities (SPLIA) and its director, Alexandra Wolfe, for her support of my book in its early stages.

I gained great insight into the local history of Nassau County by speaking with Richard Ryan of the Walt Whitman Birthplace Association; Betsey Murphy, local historian at the Jericho Public Library; Claire Bellerjeau of the Raynham Hall Museum; John Hammond, the historian for the Town of Oyster Bay; and Harry Macy, former editor of the *New York Genealogical and Biographical Record*. I appreciate all of their efforts, thoughts and correspondence with me during my time of research.

Much appreciated are the historical documents, maps and the help of the staff at the William L. Clements Library at the University of Michigan in Ann Arbor, Michigan.

Appreciation is owed to the staff of the Long Island Studies Institute at Hofstra University for assisting me in my research of the Seth Norton Papers and other relative manuscripts of the period.

A thank-you to the Oyster Bay Historical Society, the Townsend Society and the historian of the Town of Huntington for assisting and supplying local history research on the Jericho, Oyster Bay and Huntington areas.

A very special thank-you to the great efforts and assistance provided by Steve Boerner, Andrea Meyer and Gina Piastuck of the Long Island Collection at the East Hampton Library. This collection is one of the best resources for the local history of Long Island and covers both Nassau and Suffolk Counties. The staff members are very knowledgeable and helpful and provide a great effort toward future preservation and the use of documents relative to Long Island's history.

A thank-you to the staff of the Rogers Memorial Library in Southampton for their help in my research of their collection of Long Island historical documents.

I am also grateful for the assistance provided by Mary Cummings of the Southampton Historical Museum and Zach Studenroth, town historian of the Town of Southampton. They both gave insight and documentation regarding the early history of the village of Southampton.

A thank-you to Susan Mullin of the John Jermain Library in Sag Harbor, who assisted me in collecting historical records about the village of Sag Harbor in the time of the American Revolution.

I am also grateful for the study and use of the collection of historical maps that has been digitized at Stony Brook University.

A thank-you to the staff at the Brooklyn Historical Society and the Othmer Library for their assistance regarding the Henry Onderdonk Papers. Onderdonk's writings and research are truly inspiring, and the preservation of his manuscripts and scrapbooks is of great resource.

Much appreciated is the help of Imrie Risley Miniatures in providing work and information on the drawings of Clyde Risley. Risley was a master of illustrating the period and troops of the time.

Thanks also go to the the support of my personal friends. Special thanks to Michael Frisk of Stony Brook University for furthering my understanding of the maturity and growth of trees. These are great indicators of the passage of time.

A thank-you to Tracey Zabar for her support and expertise on book writing and her coaching on further author outreach.

Special thanks to William Salas of the Smithtown Public Library for his support. Thank you in advance for your assistance regarding future library outreach for the topic and the book.

I would like to thank The History Press for recognizing and supporting my interest and passion for the subject and affording me the opportunity to tell this important story. My hope is that this book is only the first step in my research of this subject in the Long Island region.

Appreciation is owed to my mother and father for taking me to all those historic sites when I was young and for creating my great curiosity for these sites and their geometries.

Lastly, a special thank-you to my loving wife, Jennifer, who supported me in all my efforts during the creation of this book.

INTRODUCTION

I have always been intrigued with the eighteenth century. In the last few years, I have had the opportunity to tour and view a number of colonial houses and structures on the East Coast of the United States. Most impressive are sites and architectural reproductions that come close to a purity or complete accuracy in their historical presentation. There is a particular charm and fascination in experiencing architecture and everyday items the way the colonials did while also beginning to understand how and why they developed these articles the way they did. I have learned that true authentic discovery of eighteenth-century architectural details requires a look beneath the surface. A study of the simplest of features in a building—such as a door or trim piece or the structure of an attic or cellar—gives us a direct link to life in our colonial past. In studying these details and understanding them, it is like learning about a whole new world—both unique and intriguing— somewhat foreign to our own. It is through this historical accuracy in re-creating or preserving sites that we are able to come closer to experiencing and understanding life in earlier times. I personally love the thrill of spending a few hours regularly incarnated in the eighteenth century.

It was through this intrigue that I set out on a personal quest to discover a lost part of the eighteenth century in my own area. This book tells the story of several Revolutionary War–era fortifications that existed on Long Island and were established by the British army in the years of the occupation (1776–83) during the American Revolution. After the fall of New York City in 1776, the occupying British forces established a defensive network of posts that secured goods sailing to New York City and provided operational bases for the foraging of supplies for the King's army in the New York area. They also provided a network of coordinated communication and early intelligence gathering points for possible Patriot raids across Long Island Sound from American-held Connecticut. After the war, the forts were abandoned or destroyed and fell into decay. Their histories and locations have been much overlooked and neglected. It has been speculated that after the Revolution, the survivors on Long Island strongly resented their former enemies. Many loathed any remembrance of this period of British occupation on Long Island and would have naturally suppressed their recollections of the fortifications and their connections to the enemy. This may explain the demise of most of the British sites over the ages.

One of the most important questions I considered in thinking about this book and why it should be written was "Why would we want to learn more about these British forts?" Interestingly, the major American cities of the the Northeast in the Revolutionary War all had networks of forts—both American and British—established across their fronts as defensive lines. These fortification lines were well recorded in large-scale campaign maps of the period. In 1776, across from Manhattan in Brooklyn, construction began on a chain of American forts, redoubts, flèches and other fortified works and posts. These included fortifications at Brooklyn Heights and the key passes through the heavily forested and thicketed Heights of Gowanus. These included Fort Stirling at the waterfront, Fort Corkscrew (Cobble Hill) and a chain of works comprising Fort Greene, Fort Box, Fort Putnam and the Oblong Redoubt. There were also several smaller entrenchments and earthwork lines linking the forts together.[1] The remnants of these inner-city forts—such as at Brooklyn—were lost long ago due to the growth of our eastern Mid-Atlantic urban areas. Development won out over preservation of these historical sites in our cities.

The chain of British forts on Long Island had many similarities to all of these inner-city forts—with variations in scale and situation based on local geography. The British and early American fortifications were designed and built according to European principles and adapted to the context and landscape of North America. Many American engineers fought for the British prior to the American Revolution and learned their art engaged in or studying about these fortifications in earlier colonial wars. Most of the Long Island forts were also built and garrisoned by Loyalist forces—colonists who remained loyal to the Crown. The British relied almost totally on earthen embankment construction in their forts. Many of the American forts around

Johnston Map showing chain of American fortifications at Brooklyn in 1776. *From Henry P. Johnston's 1878 edition of* The Campaign of 1776 around New York and Brooklyn.

New York City and along the Hudson River were faced with wood for their defensive walls. This difference in material seems to be one of the acute contrasts in the engineering preferences of the opposing armies.

Today, Long Island's twenty-first-century development is rapidly expanding, but there are still enough actual ruins of these forts that further research can still be done. This book would like to take advantage of this pause in time long enough to elaborate on the story of these lost forts. The book wishes to focus on the fortified posts outside of modern-day New York City and those sites that were east of the town of Jamaica, New York, on Long Island.

It is in recognizing the loss of those inner-city posts lining our great Revolutionary cities that we can begin to appreciate the fading of these important Long Island historic sites. The remaining forts on Long Island will probably not withstand the test of time much longer. It is the hope that with this volume of additional research we may come to learn more about the architectural works of all of the revolutionaries—both American and British—of the period.

Historically, British field fortifications were made in consideration of the circumstances of survival and warfare in revolutionary times. The reconciliation with an ancient wilderness and the need for wartime defense became primary objectives of the period. Fortifications were established on high points of land and provided access to waterways and major roadways. Sites were selected with an understanding of defense and the knowledge of artillery trajectories, along with a local understanding of available materials and methods of construction. On Long Island, the hilly landscape of the northern shore—combined with its natural water inlets and harbors off the sound—made this prime landscape for establishing the greatest number of British posts. Taking full advantage of these natural features, they utilized

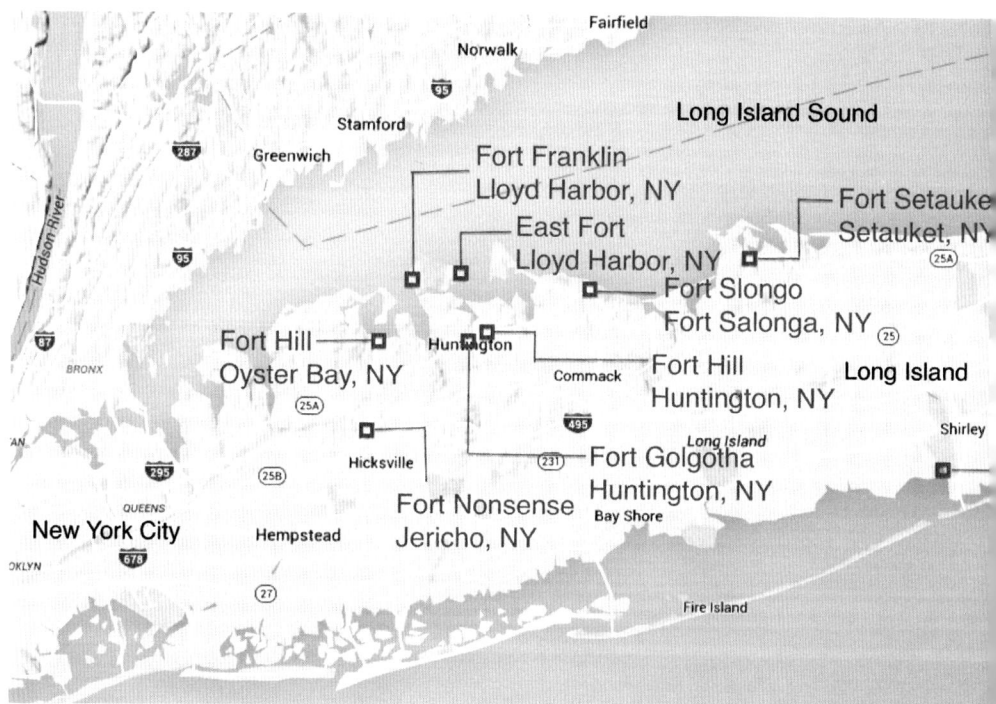

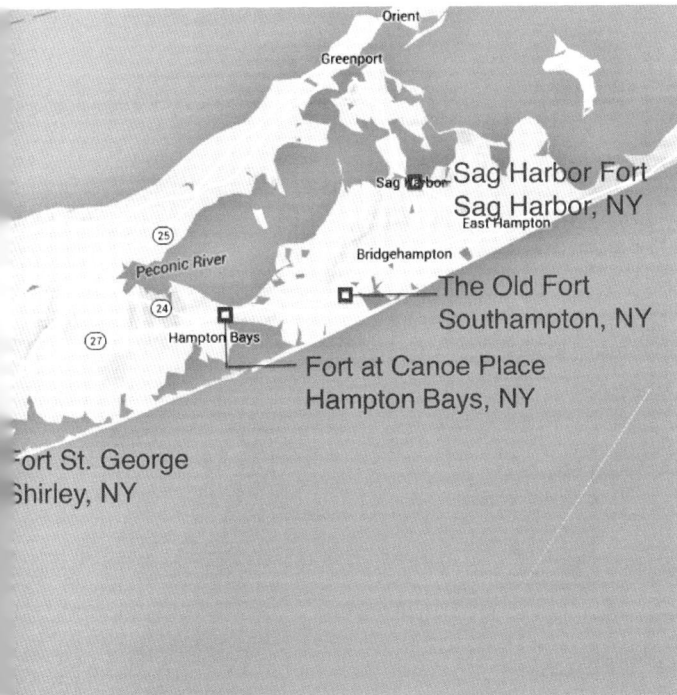

Top: Close-up of a view of the Rebel works around Walton's House, with Hell Gate and the island. *From* Archibald Robertson: His Diaries and Sketches in America 1762–1780. *New York Public Library Digital Collections.*

Left: The network of British forts on occupied Long Island during the American Revolution. *Map by the author.*

this landscape to its full potential in establishing their defensive posts. These forts were in all a vernacular architecture born out of a primal need for defense. At the time, war was not only about fighting the enemy but also about surviving the hardships of the natural wilderness. The need for survival became necessary to both the occupied and the occupier.

This general study of the fortifications of Long Island articulates written histories and through a research of both recorded maps and a field study of the actual sites strives to piece together some of the realities and myths of these historical sites. These small forts or redoubts were contrived, for the most part, of pure geometries dictated by eighteenth-century British colonial engineering. The first chapter of the book will explain the eighteenth-century redoubt in its historical context and from a British engineering standpoint. It will also explain how guidelines were suited to the American landscape. The next twelve chapters will dwell on each of the known and recorded fort sites, telling their histories in the context of the American Revolution on Long Island. The chapters will also give background research into their historical location and any architectural remains or discovered facts yielding to their existence. Lastly, the chapters will touch on any preservation initiatives that have aided in allowing their remains to survive into the present day.

With the loss of these historical constructions due mostly to suburban development and the ongoing weathering of the ages, the rediscovery of the sites is as much a research into the very notions that created them. Studies of geography, topography and specific local histories mixed with an analysis of professional period manuals for the design of fortifications all help in making assumptions and speculations about these historical sites. The author, through the help of period resources, will present conjectural mappings of some of the lesser known sites, giving us another view into the Revolutionary War period.

With the recent success and interest in books such as *Washington's Spies: The Story of America's First Spy Ring*, by Alexander Rose, and AMC's *TURN*, a TV series about the Culper Spy Ring on Long Island, we see a new generation of interest in the Revolutionary War period. Along with this new interest in the period, this work really wishes to set apart fiction from reality. With its research of actual historic places, even some featured in the book and TV series, the reader can learn more about the history of Long Island during this interesting time of its history. The visualization of the British headquarters in Setauket in the TV series *TURN* is portrayed as a rudimentary fortification at the village church. In fact, the reality of this fortification is somewhat different. There were very disciplined design principles utilized in fortifying and defending a building or church and ensuring the ultimate defense of the commanders and troops posted there. The fort would have architecturally displayed a dominance of the position, and its physical appearance would have supported that in every way.

It is my hope that the text and research will appeal to both the general reader and those more scholarly, such as military historians, architectural historians, landscape architects, historic preservationists and general history enthusiasts. In the spirit of Robert B. Robert's important book *New York's Forts in the Revolution* (Fairleigh Dickinson University Press, 1980), my book wishes to elaborate and expand on his chapter regarding the Long Island forts, telling a more up-to-date and site specific history of all the British posts in the time of the occupation. It really takes a book to tell their story. I think the work will be a positive addition to many people's historical collections and strike a new interest in an upcoming generation intrigued by the Revolutionary War, shedding new light on both American and British early colonial architecture.

Note: Transcribed quotations appear in the book in their original form as documented from sources. Any errors in spelling and grammar are characteristic of the language of the period and are transcribed exactly as recorded.

1

THE REDOUBT IN EIGHTEENTH-CENTURY AMERICA

*T*his chapter will give technical background for the development of field fortifications and their evolution in eighteenth-century America. The field fortification was defined in Lewis Lochee's *Elements of Field Fortifications* as "the art of constructing such temporary works, either in woods or open fields, or for the occasional defence of houses, churches, castles, villages and small towns, as will enable the men within to withstand a greater number without."[2] The North American field fortification was typically built in remote locations using local and readily accessible materials such as lumber and earth. The forts were naturally temporal works, their materials of an impermanent nature. All of the British fortifications on Long Island were of this temporary type as described by Lewis Lochee.

The selection of a site for a fort was influenced by several factors both strategic and tactical. One of the most common requirements was the site's need for proximity to vital transportation routes. This meant forts were most commonly established adjacent to waterways and important roadways. Access to water for the defending force's use and hygiene along with an unlimited access to fuel (wood) for fires were both key factors in determining a fort's location.[3]

The site for a fortification was selected by a senior military commander who acted on his determination of what might be best for the operations of his command in that particular region. A senior engineer would advance this determination by making recommendations for a location of tactical

Major Archibald Robertson in the uniform of the Corps of Royal Engineers, 1782. Portrait by George Romney. *Courtesy of the Museum of Fine Arts, St. Petersburg, Florida.*

advantage that would limit the number of possible threats against it. This included an analysis of the most tactical advantage the topography could afford. Also important was to consider the type of weapons that might be directed against the fort. Both of these elements influenced the siting and layout of the fortifications and the manner and characteristics of its construction.

In designing the fort, the engineer or ranking officer commonly prepared a map showing the location of the site in the context of its topography.[4] Major Archibald Robertson, a high-ranking engineer, wrote a diary of his years of service in the British army in America between 1762 and 1780. In reading through his diary, it can be seen that he traveled extensively with the high command around New York City and visited many of the fortification sites on Long Island, giving directions and recommendations to these posts.[5]

Before moving onto greater detail of the specifics of the forts, it is also important to mention briefly another engineering principle referred to as *commanding ground*. A height of land was always of advantage in positioning a fort in the landscape, but it was equally advantageous for the site to be located in proximity of ground higher than that of the fortified site. In the eighteenth century, cannons could fire in a direct line from the commanding elevation and totally threaten the position of any lower positions. There seemed to be some controversy over the required distance a position needed to be located from superior commanding ground, but the accepted norm was the requirement of six hundred yards.[6] It was also accepted that the most dangerous exposure to a commanding height was on the reverse or rear side.[7]

The most common type of military fortification utilized in the period was the *redoubt*. The redoubt was enclosed on all sides and thus effectively became its own small independent fort to secure a guard or post. Its size was proportionate to the number of men meant to defend it. Redoubts had different plans and profiles, and their form was determined by that which was most appropriate for the ground on which they were to be established.[8]

Traditionally, in Europe, the redoubt was used in common with larger masonry fortifications and placed in outworks to defend critical points and support the larger fortification as a whole.[9] In America, redoubts were for the most part built as standalone fortifications similar to those described by Lochee. All of the redoubts on Long island were standalone works similar to this type.

Most of the redoubts of the period were square in plan. Lochee described how different shapes could also be used:

> *The redoubt had no precise or common form, but may be a square, a rhombus, a trapezium, a trapezoid, a pentagon either regular or irregular, a circle or any other form. The form is indeed, determined by the spot of ground on which it is raised, and the purposes for which it is constructed. When there is no essential reason to the contrary, the form is commonly a square.*[10]

The concept of the *regular* fortification was accepted as a general ideal in the manuals of the time in order to minimize variability in a fort's strength. The *irregular* fortification suited the nature of the topography of the American colonies, creating essential differences in its sides and the strength of these sides. Engineers of the period strived for the principles of regular as opposed to irregular, as the former were all the more perfect and came closer to the ideal balancing of the art of them.[11]

According to Playdell, "The chief care in tracing out a redoubt, should be to examine thoroughly which is the quarter the most exposed, or where the enemy can make the easiest approach."[12] He goes on to say that the side of easiest approach should not be defended by any oblique angle of the work but with a direct face or side—thus giving a more direct line of fire to defenders. He also explains via a diagram the principles of a fortification that were meant to defend the passage of a roadway through a valley. One face of the redoubt was meant to be established pointing directly at the angle of the direct approach of a passage. This passage was also directed to be within musket shot distance of the redoubt, or about three hundred yards. All sides of the fort were also to be cleared of woods or growth from the height of the redoubt to the bottom of its hill. He adds that this clearing needed to be at least five hundred paces around on all sides of the works.

Playdell's manual also lays out a clear dimensional guide to aid in designing and determining a redoubt's size. He describes that an ordinary pace of two feet was equivalent to each rank and file of a defender and each file was to be two-men deep. Thus a banquette of a redoubt twenty paces in length could present a front of twenty men. Forty men total could be presented if two ranks deep. This would be equivalent to a modern dimension of forty feet of frontage on each side. He also adds that when cannons were intended to be placed in the work, then six paces should be allotted for a field piece and eight paces for a twelve-pounder. Finally, he determined that the least interior circumference that should be in a square redoubt is eighty paces total or twenty paces on each of its four sides. This was intended to aid its defenders in not feeling overcrowded during the defense of the position. It was also intended to limit an attacker's potential ability to use a single grenade to destroy a significant number of the defending force.

The entrance to a redoubt needed to be situated on the face of the redoubt least exposed to possible attack. It was to be five paces wide if cannons were to be used. If no cannons were to be used, three or four paces would suffice.[13]

The specific design details of a redoubt had characteristics that could easily be transcribed onto other fort sites. Even as these initial guidelines

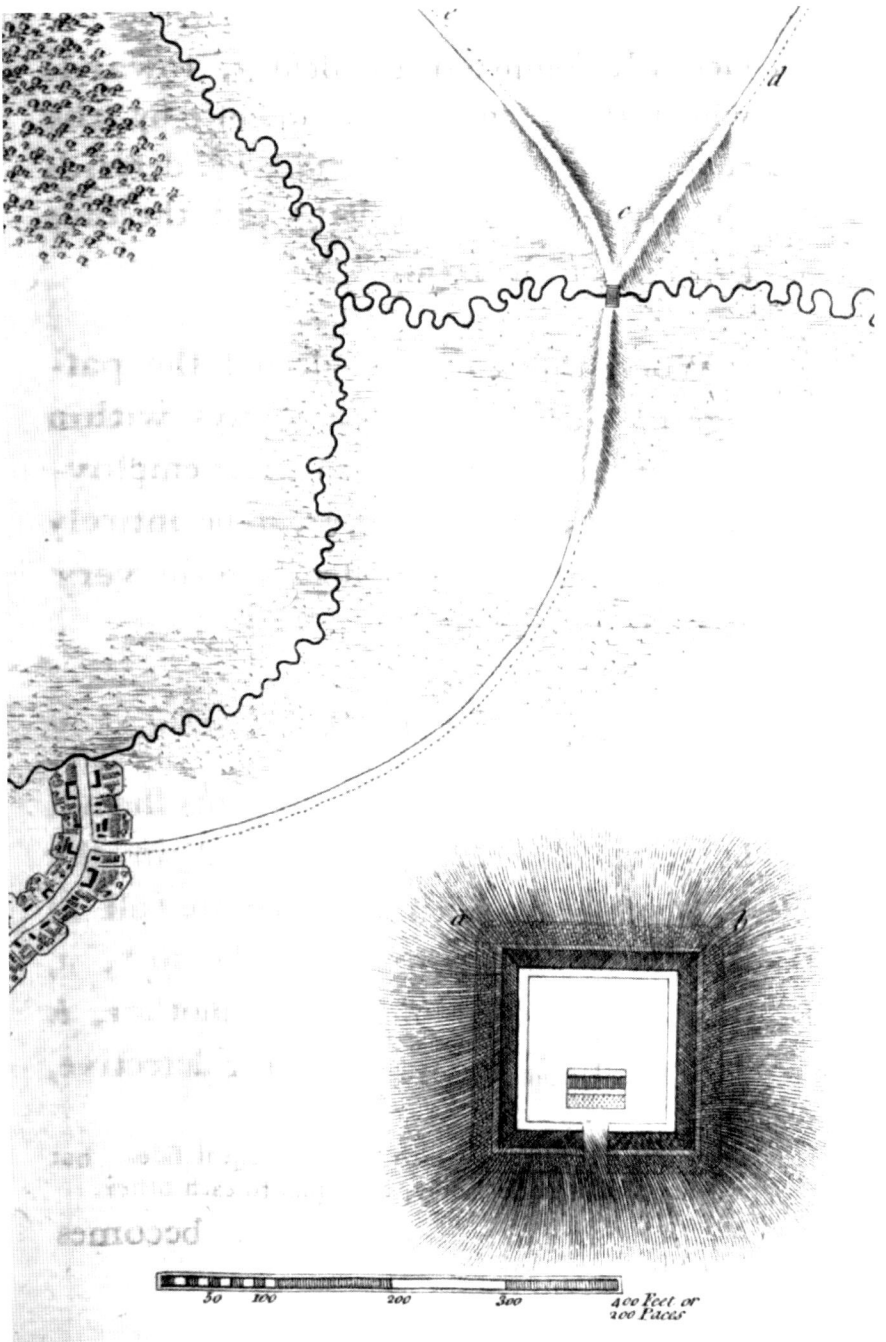

Plan of a redoubt. *From "An Essay on Field Fortification: Intended Principally for the Use of Officers of Infantry," by J.C. Pleydell, 1768.*

were theoretical in nature, the engineers of the period were trained to aspire toward the attributes of the regular work.

One of the most important aspects of the redoubt was the earthwork component composed of the *parapet, banquette* and *ditch.* According to Lochee, "The parapet is the bank of earth surrounding the post to be defended, and covers the troops and artillery employed for its defense."[14] As earth was a more favorable material than stone and wood in absorption of artillery impact, the depth of the parapet could be determined based on the threat of the musketry or cannonade attack. The range of dimension at the top of the parapet was between two to seven feet deep, and this difference was the variable between a musket and a twelve-pounder heavy cannon shot. The height of the parapet was to be at least six feet tall to properly cover the men inside. The banquette was an elevated platform on the back side of the parapet from which the men could stand and fire. Its standard dimension was approximately four and a half feet from the top of the parapet. The depth of the banquette front to back was also typically four and a half feet so that defenders had room enough to stand two-men deep.[15]

A ditch surrounded the redoubt on all sides directly outside of the parapet and was sometimes referred to as the *fosse.* It was meant to increase the difficulty of the approach of the attacking force and also supplied the earth necessary for building the parapet berm. According to Lochee, the depth of the ditch was never to be less than six feet deep. The slope nearest the parapet was the *scarp* and the slope farthest from it the *counterscarp.* Between the parapet and the scarp was a small section of horizontal earth that prevented the earth from sliding down from the parapet and into the ditch. This section was referred to as the *berme* or berm. The berm was further strengthened using *fraizing*—horizontal and pointed stakes that were directed outward from the fort. The stakes lined the berm close together to inhibit anyone from penetrating between them, and they were slightly inclined downward with the use of sleepers underneath. The stakes formed a type of broken shelf, but their incline down and outward helped to defend if grenades were thrown in or out of the redoubt. The grenade would roll back into the ditch and onto any attackers.[16] The stakes would have to be hacked with axes to breach these works and ascend to the parapet of the fort.

Likewise, Lochee also suggested that *palisades* could also be utilized to give additional defense to the redoubt. Palisades were poles of a strong wood three to four inches thick that were pointed at the end, partially buried and set vertically in the ground. They were fastened to a horizontal rail and together formed a wall of sorts that could surround a post or be set at the

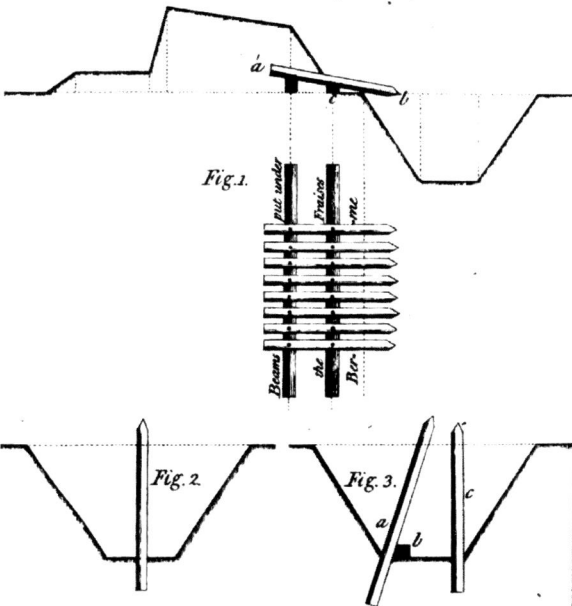

Left: Cross-sections through parapet and ditch. *From "An Essay on Field Fortification: Intended Principally for the Use of Officers of Infantry," by J.C. Pleydell, 1768.*

Below: The assault on redoubt no. 10 at the Battle of Yorktown. From a painting by H. Charles McBarron. *Wikimedia Commons.*

bottom of the ditch.[17] At Yorktown, Virginia, a replica of a British redoubt of the time clearly shows that palisades were utilized in the approach to the fort by the ditch.

The last line of outbound defense in the construction of a redoubt was an *abbatis*—a circumference of felled trees set outside the ditch that were laid horizontally with their branches set outward toward a possible attacking force. An abbatis could render very efficient defense by placing the trees close to one another and intertwining the branches. This could delay attackers by entangling them and allowing the defending force to fire directly on them.[18] Notwithstanding the fact that Long Island in the Revolutionary War was highly wooded, almost all of the redoubts recorded on the island in this period utilized an abbatis, thus also demonstrating that it was a highly effective means for defense.

If cannons were used in conjunction with the redoubt, they were commonly set on platforms within the work, and *embrasures* (openings) were cut into the parapet to allow the artillery to be fired from behind this protection. Some redoubts allowed the cannons to be fired over the parapet wall, but this was all dependent on the size and height of the artillery piece and the embankment.[19]

A defense element that is not as well covered in the field fortification manuals of the period but was heavily utilized at the Long Island fortifications was the *blockhouse*. It is recorded that many of the posts had blockhouses, and some had as many as two of them within their walls. The blockhouse was an independent fortified building—heavily constructed of timber logs—oftentimes two stories high. It would be encircled with apertures to allow defending fire from within. Sometimes a cannon could be mounted inside the blockhouse. The second story would typically overhang the lower story so that defenders could use their muskets to fire down against any attacker who came close and under its overhang. The blockhouse also became a secondary defensive post within the redoubt if the outer fort's walls were breached. Sometimes, a blockhouse also doubled as troop barracks or was used as a storehouse.[20] As previously mentioned, the forts of Long Island were all essentially single standalone redoubts. It can only be assumed that due to the limited size of these forts, the blockhouse was a positive addition, contributing strength and needed troop quartering space to the post.

For the sake of comparison, many of the American fortifications closer to New York City and in the uplands of the Hudson Valley utilized similar principles but relied much more on wood construction for their

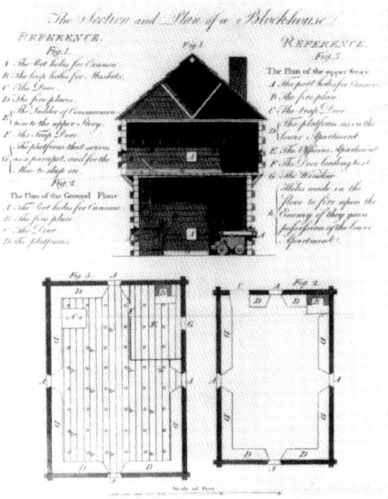

"The Section and Plan of a Blockhouse." *From* Anburey's Travels Through
the Interior Parts of America, *vol. I
(London, 1789).*

battlements. The engineers and
soldiers would build a framework
of interlocking hewn logs and fill
them with dirt. In other forts, they
would also use *fascines*, which were
tightly bound bundles of sticks.
They would pile them up along
their embankments.[21] This type
of construction can be seen in the
drawings of Rebel fortifications
surrounding New York City within
the diary of Archibald Robertson of
the Royal Engineers. The American
positions along the Hudson River, at
Fort's Montgomery and near Clinton
also utilized these construction
methods. Although it seems this
method was preferred or commonly
used, its initial origin was British.
The early British fort at what later became Fort Stanwix in Upstate New
York was built years before the Revolution and utilized this method of
wooden construction.

As many of the forts to be covered in this book were established to
strengthen a post within a village or town, it is also relevant to consider
the elements recommended to ensure the defense of villages. Specific
circumstances of village defense will be touched on in later chapters, but
a short summary of the general principles of defense will be made here.
In *Elements of Field Fortification*, Lewis Lochee included a section titled "Of
Fortifying Villages":

> *The side of the village towards the enemy, should be fortified with works
> of earth raised at some distance from the houses, that if they catch fire, the
> heat may not oblige the men to abandon the works, which should be cannon-
> proof, and may either be detached or continued.*[22]

He advises that the primary and main objectives are to allow the
entrenchments to flank (be beside) one another and prevent the works
being turned on one side or the other. If there is not sufficient time to raise
earthworks, the houses nearest the approaches of possible attack should be

put in a defensive state—especially where the roads meet. He further suggests that the intervals between the houses should be barricaded or strengthened with works and that the advanced guards and outposts need to be established in their proper places to help deter an element of surprise by the enemy.[23] According to Gross, the main guard oversaw three to six small outposts and was placed upon the most important posts, roads or openings of the area.[24]

Likewise, the advanced guard positions needed to be at the front of the defensive line of the post to alert the positions farther back in the line. It seems that regular patrols also kept a watch over the area and the boundaries of the post, keeping it somewhat secure. In the First Battalion of Maryland Loyalists' orderly book can be seen the written commands concerning an active post on Long Island. The orderly book captures a period in the year 1778 in which combined Loyalist forces made a sequence of movements and post establishments across Long Island. They moved from the west end of the island to the east end and out along the North Fork and back again to New York City. Here we are able to learn of the establishment of temporary camp position points such as Setauket, Miller Place, Wading River and Mattituck. Mattituck seemed to be a significant and important position. It was extensively guarded with advanced positions and patrols.[25] A map of the period also shows that it had many defensive features and positive elements in supporting its force. It seems Mattituck's occupation was planned to be temporary, and it did not attain a longtime standing as a strategic position. There is no record of physical fortifications being built there.

The village of Hempstead—approximately twenty miles out of New York City on the south shore of Long Island—was also a large British camp and winter troop quarters during the years of the Revolution. The position was termed an outpost, and soldiers and sentries are recorded as being positioned for miles around it. The Seventeenth Light Dragoons were stationed for periods within the village. From Hempstead, they were able to forage on the Hempstead Plains, and the village was also near enough to New York City in case an attack there needed their support. The Presbyterian church in the village was used as a barracks for soldiers and, later in the war, as a riding school for drilling horses.[26] There are no records of Hempstead having been fortified at the time, so this post is not covered as a chapter in this book.

In the Revolutionary War, the British and American forces also utilized a series of signal fires to act as long-range beacons to warn and command naval forces and ground troops. The British had this system in place on the northern shore of Long Island. A period map of the fort at Lloyd's Neck shows the position of the beacons in that particular area.

With the advancement of fortification engineering highlighted above and through a thorough study of relevant period manuals, it can be understood that a very sophisticated series of principles in fort establishment had already been developed by the late eighteenth century in America. British forces in the Revolutionary War on Long Island utilized these principles to full effect. No one will doubt that these constructions displayed a disciplined and systematic mastering of the local region and its environment. By means of their physical appearance, the forts assured the local population of their commanding dominance over the landscape and their individual regions, respectively.

2

FORT NONSENSE

JERICHO, NEW YORK

Jericho was the first village east of Jamaica that had a British fortification established within its boundaries. The village of Jericho had a number of forked roads at its center that radiated out in all directions: east, west, north and south. Jericho was also located along the main road from New York through Jamaica and leading to the village of Oyster Bay and the British post there. There are accounts of Jericho being fortified with a British construction called Fort Nonsense. There are a few different thoughts on the origin of the name for the fort to this day. Its history is lacking, and the fort's remembrance has somewhat vanished from local memory. It may have been considered so insignificant at the time that its name passed down as Fort Nonsense. It may not have existed at all. There is enough period reference to verify that a fortified British outpost did exist in Jericho at the time. Evidence is lacking on the layout of the village at the time of the Revolution. Due to the mystery surrounding its past and the extent of Jericho's modern-day redevelopment, it has been the most difficult of all the forts on Long Island to research.

Jericho is labeled on at least two period maps, indicating its location as a post for British forces on Long Island in the Revolutionary War. In a call to raise men by local Loyalist units in March 1778, Jericho is referred to as a recruitment station.[27] In a 1778 orderly book of the Maryland Loyalist Regiment, the post was referred to as "Camp Jericho." The regiment was on its way east when this entry was made in July 1778.[28] The record states very little about the extent of the Jericho camp at this time.

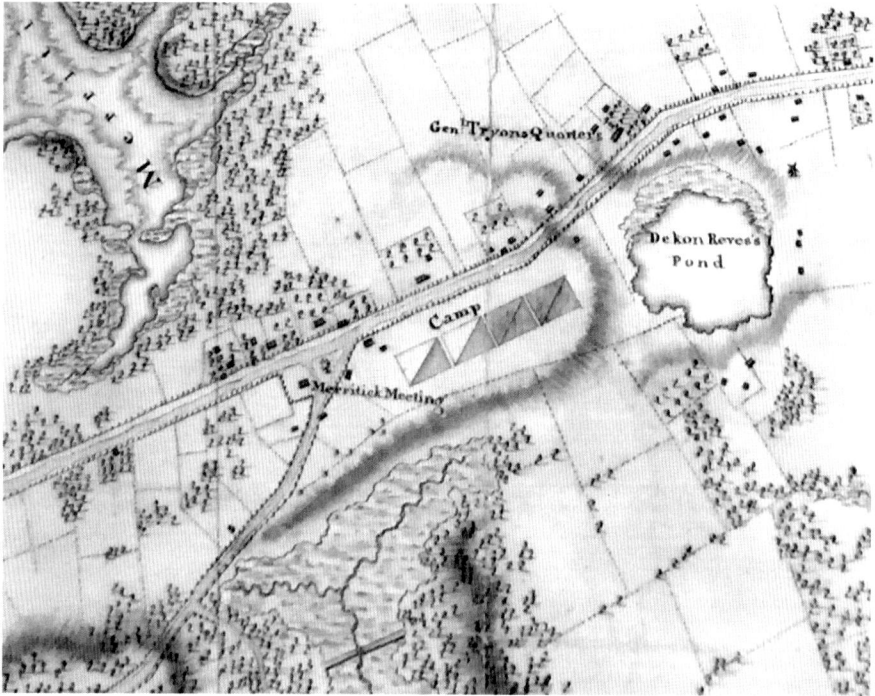

A plan of Mattituck in the township of Southold on Long Island, 1778, by Samuel Holland. *Courtesy of the William L. Clements Library, the University of Michigan, Ann Arbor, Michigan.*

A map of a British and Loyalist camp—farther out on Long Island at Mattituck—from the same period shows a linear arrangement to an encampment that was established there. It is positioned along the main road near a fork in the road and situated on an elevated piece of land near a small pond. The map shows the commander's headquarters farther east along the roadway and opposite the main camp. It is also positioned on a small height of land.

There is more evidence that the post at Jericho was established some time between October and November 1778 as a winter quarters for part of the British forces of Oyster Bay and a central location for the dispatching of units on foraging patrols. In a letter from early November addressed to a Seth Norton, who was an assistant commissary (forage master) for the Loyalist troops, it requested he was to proceed to Jericho and take charge and supply forage to the horses of the British Legion and the troops quartered at that post.[29] The British Legion was a combined cavalry and infantry unit established by Lord Cathcart in 1778 and made up of Loyalist recruits from New York, Pennsylvania and New Jersey. In 1778, the Legion infantry was under the direct command of Major Cochrane. Lieutenant Colonel Banastre Tarleton commanded the cavalry unit, which eventually gained the name "Tarleton's Legion." The infantry and cavalry units were notorious for their brutality toward the civilian populations on Long Island at the time. The Legion went on to fight many battles throughout the southern campaigns of the war and returned to Long Island in later periods to take winter quarters.

In November 1778, the cavalry component of the Legion was present in Jericho.[30] It was the perfect location for the Legion cavalry, as the village center was situated on somewhat of an open plain with several farm clearings surrounding it. It also granted direct access to the flatter lands along the middle of Long Island and the Hempstead Plains directly to the south. Ranging the countryside on horseback collecting supplies was ideal for the experience and training of the troops. In a February 1779 letter dispatch, Lieutenant Donald McCrummin of the Legion reported about foraging activities of the cavalry and the buying of hay in Jericho.[31] As he was an officer of the infantry component of the Legion, this confirms that in all probability there were detachments of both mounted and infantry troops present in Jericho.

Onderdonk's book *Incidents of Queens County* gives the most compelling evidence that the troops of the Legion had created Fort Nonsense. He makes reference to a newspaper article of December 10, 1778, that reports Long Island British troops were building huts or barracks at Jericho. He added a footnote: "The Legion lay at Jericho, and built a fort called Fort Nonsense, on a hill around Dr. Townsend's barn."[32]

A surveillance letter of November 10, 1778, from a Brigadier Charles Scott to General Washington read as follows:

> *I this moment reed a letter from Capt. Leavenworth who is from long Island this morning. He informs me that Sir William Easkin with 350 horse and 300 infantry is at Jeric[h]o on long Island, he has Turnd the Inhabitance out of dors to Barrack his troops, and is throwing up Works round Doctr Townsends Hous where he him Self Quarters, he tells the people that he is to winter there, but the inhabitance thinks his business there is only to Forrage, which they have begun very Rapidly.*[33]

The foraging of the force was also noted in Onderdonk's book: "Zopher Platt's ox-team was pressed by Major Cochran (under Col. Tarlton), to carry boards ripped off his barn from Huntington to Jericho. The Major also took 40 lbs. of butter from his wife, and carried all to Col. Tarlton's quarters, without pay."[34]

With these accounts, it becomes clear that Jericho was significant as a passage point between Jamaica and Oyster Bay and, due to its cavalry component, was a quartering and foraging station for the region.

In starting to put together a speculation of the possible location and use of the post at Jericho, it is interesting to consider period manuals that discuss the guidelines for establishing outposts for the housing of small bodies of infantry and cavalry and defining a front of defense. One of these manuals, *Duties of an Officer in the Field*, by Baron Gross—albeit of a slightly later period— highlights the instructions for infantry and cavalry units in locating and fortifying themselves in a series of posts, advanced posts and stations of the main guard.

Illustration of a trooper, the British Legion (Tarleton's), 1779. *Courtesy of K/S Historical Publications and Imrie/Risley Miniatures.*

In the chapter describing the posting of guards of the infantry, he begins by defining the locations needed for the advanced guards and the main guard. He elaborates on the necessity of the advanced guards to be used in the reconnoitering of roads, passes and defiles between the stations and for limiting access between them and the enemy. The distance between posts is directed as to be about two hundred paces from one another. This rule is somewhat dependent on the ground on which they are positioned. Furthermore, he states that the main guard should be placed upon the most important posts, roads or openings and the advanced guard positions are dependent on the main guard post. This main guard position usually had a commanding officer present. He concludes that the main guard was to be covered by an abattis or parapet and possibly supported by cannon.[35]

Likewise, Baron Gross's guidelines state that the main guard and outposts of cavalry are most commonly stationed in open plains. He refers to the stations as *vedettes*, which were to be placed at passes and other such points that were favorable for observing and protecting the site from the enemy. He adds that these vedettes were to be four hundred to five hundred paces

from one another. If the country were hilly, posts should be stationed on the summits of high points and woods used to conceal them if under attack.[36] It is unclear if the post at Jericho was established as a series of posts for infantry or cavalry in much the same fashion as these guidelines attest. As the next chapter on Oyster Bay will exhibit, a map of the time does show a similar network of advanced fortified positions that surrounded the central redoubt, which was on the dominating height of the area. No dominating or defensive high position is recorded or noted in Jericho during or after the period of the Revolution. This dominating position, if it could be found, may in fact be the historical location of Fort Nonsense—if it existed at all. Time and development have managed to conceal most clues.

In the 1970s, members of Nassau County Museum did some site and ground research of the area for possible fortified hill sites. They did a ground analysis of the property around the presumed location of the Dr. James Townsend property, later to be the Malcolm property. Today, the site is the property of the Malcolm Jackson House, at the apex of Old Jericho Turnpike and the old roads leading to Oyster Bay and Cedar Swamp. The grounds of the property showed no identifiable remains of fortified hill positions. It was also speculated at that time that the large Underhill property west of the cloverleaf and modern routes 106 and 107 could also be the site of a fortified position, as this property once belonged to the Townsend family

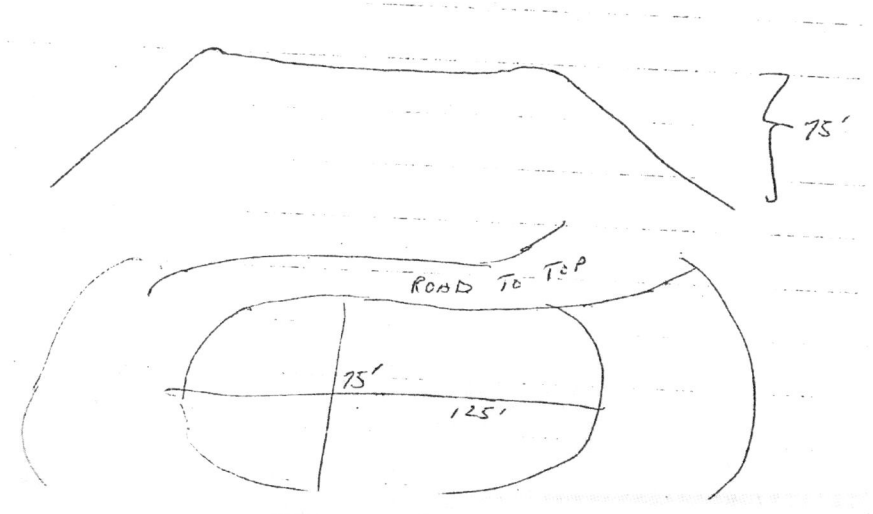

Sketch of a hill at the Harold Underhill farm in Jericho by Richard Ryan, 1977. *Courtesy of the Jericho Public Library.*

during the Revolution. The site analysis recorded that there was a hill of strategic merits located on the property; its top was approximately 75 feet above the surrounding area and afforded significant views of the region. It was recorded that the sides of the hill were steep—at about a forty-five-degree angle—and the top of the hill had a flattened area of approximately 75 feet by 125 feet.[37] After analyzing the location of this hill, the author concluded that the height of land no longer exists and it was bulldozed in the building of a housing development on a section of the Underhill property during the 1990s.

Through an analysis of records, period troop returns, written histories and a study of land deeds of the time, the author has been able to put together his own conjecture as to the layout of the British post in Jericho during the Revolutionary War period. The above noted surveillance letters and histories of Onderdonk have convinced this author that the center of the post was located on the present-day Malcolm Jackson House property. Two accounts state that works or fortifications were located on the Dr. James Townsend property. A deed of 1795 for the land from Dr. James Townsend's widow confirms that it was sold to John Jackson in that year, and the written specifics of the surveyed land are congruent to the location and size of the location and boundaries of the present Malcolm Jackson property. The 1795 document also describes that this home lot comprised the house and barn and goes on to describe the north and east boundary lines, listing the names of the neighbors and their general locations. The deed also describes a lot across from the property in the vicinity of the present-day Malcolm Barn and ruins. A small portion of a later barn still stands today on this lot.[38]

Today, there is a small back building structure attached to the historic Malcolm Jackson House on the property. Due to some of its eighteenth-century details, there is a good chance that this structure existed partially at the time of the Revolutionary War and was either attached to the main house as a rear ell (addition) or was, in fact, the original house of Dr. James Townsend. Historically, in some other period houses of the time, additions were built to accommodate the kitchen and its accessory spaces. This would have been done so that the kitchen of the main house might be used as a dining room. Other architectural precedents from the time suggest that the rear ell structure was very often the older structure. In some cases, the rear structure was moved to the new position, and in others, it had remained in its historic location and was occupied by the household during the construction of the main house.[39]

View of the back ell section of the existing Malcolm Jackson House today, Jericho, New York. *Photo by the author.*

Interestingly, a return from 1783 listing troops housed in Jericho shows large numbers of Hessian soldiers being quartered in local homes, giving the names of the specific owners of each house and the numbers of soldiers and the rooms that were occupied. James Townsend was shown to house one lieutenant. John Carpenter's property accommodated a main guard, one lieutenant and a *piquet* (advanced guard).[40] Property deeds confirm his property was at the apex of the old Cedar Swamp Road and the road to Oyster Bay. This location confirms him as a neighbor of Dr. James Townsend; Carpenter's property was directly northwest of Townsend's plot.[41] The advanced guard piquet position directly to the northwest confirms the centrality of the Dr. James Townsend property. The main guard position at Carpenter's property would designate the entry point to Jericho from the north and makes sense with the enemy front being toward the north, or the Long Island Sound. There was likely a piquet or advanced post farther east along the Jericho Turnpike and past the location of William Seaman's homestead. Seaman is noted as the eastern neighbor of Dr. James Townsend in the 1795 deed. This would be the entry point to the post from

37

the northeast. A simple review of the roads adjacent to the property and their culmination in the strong forked intersection at Townsend's property on Old Jericho Road all stress the importance of this site, it being at the center of the village.

An analysis by the author of the actual ground and a study of topographic maps of the Malcolm Jackson property show that the southernmost portion of these grounds—where the present historic house stands—is the highest elevation of land in the vicinity. This lot, combined with the area of the Friends' meetinghouse property to the south, forms somewhat of a level plain. The land directly northeast of the Malcolm Jackson House drops away slightly, creating a raised arc or platform of land in the area of the old homestead. This plain is also level with the present Malcolm Barn property across the road and to the west. Here again the land drops away to the southwest. On studying other period surveys from the area, the original and historical Townsend barn of the time of the Revolution was probably adjacent to the original house. This would set it close to the existing house on the raised area of land. The barn most likely adjoined the house and was set close to one of the roadways for easy access. Similarly, for the caretaking of any animals, it makes sense that the barn would have been close to the house.

The speculation by this author is that the general area of the Malcolm Jackson House may have been the position of the fortified work. It could have been an earthwork or redoubt with a ditch and an abbatis directly around the James Townsend house, somewhat similar to that stated in the surveillance letter earlier. As many of the British forts on Long Island attested, a redoubt in either the form of a regular square or an irregular form could have been the same type used here. The post could also have been a combination of fortified outpost with a headquarters and an adjacent troop camp.

With the British Legion cavalry known to have been present, the barn most likely did act as a stable and could also have been fortified as noted. The level plain allowed easy access for the cavalry and a large enough area for their use. The plain—cleared of woods—dropped off in all directions and would have allowed expansive views of the countryside. What may have appeared at the time to have been a fortified headquarters at the farmhouse connected to an adjacent fortified barn for troops and horses could have appeared somewhat nonsensical to the local inhabitants. This could also explain another possible origin for the name Fort Nonsense. It could also be speculated that the name originated from the local inhabitants. Being

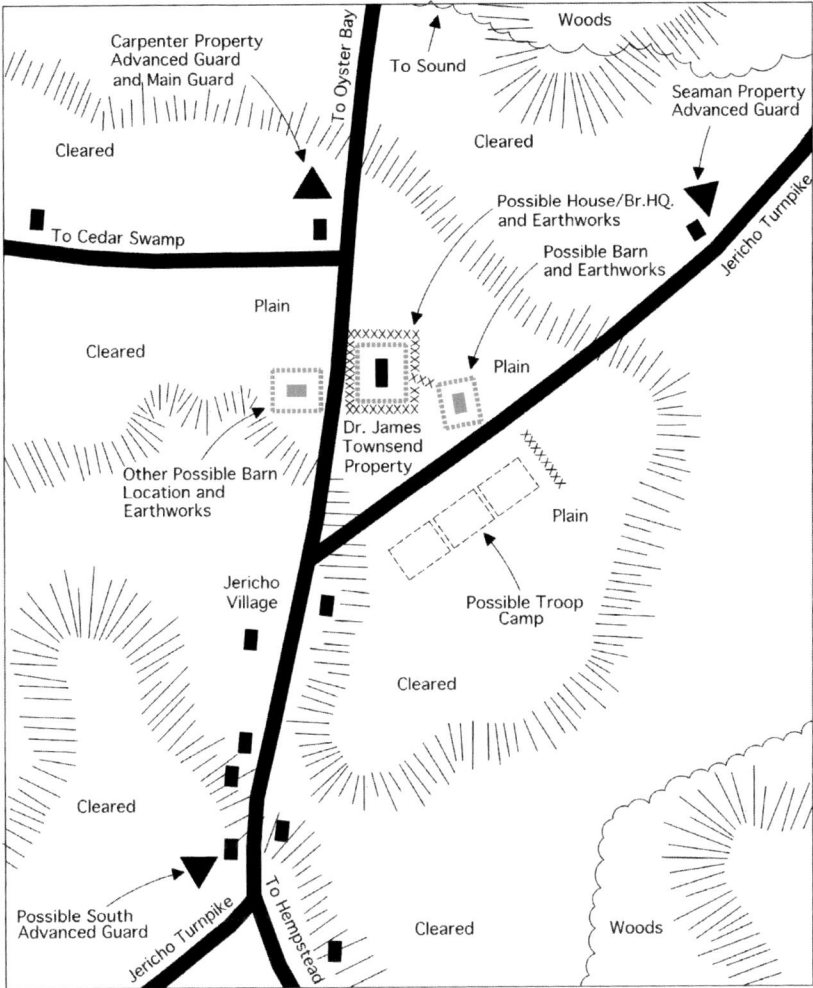

Conjectural map of Jericho in the Revolutionary War period, 1778–79. *Map by the author.*

peace-loving Quakers, they could have thought a fort was not necessary due to their pacifism in regards to the war.

Luckily, the center of Jericho and all of the Malcolm Jackson property is now a part of a twenty-acre Jericho Historic Preserve established by Nassau County in 1974 to save historic homes in their original locations.[42] The center of the village of Jericho was ripped apart by road redevelopments in the mid-twentieth century after World War II. Homes were leveled due to infrastructure work, and these exploits have created a great loss of the earlier village's fabric and character. It has also made it difficult to piece together the early morphology of the center of Old Jericho. With the preserve established indefinitely, future generations may discover the beginnings of Jericho. As for Fort Nonsense, the preserve allows the myth to live on, with the possible chance that someday its historic remains may finally be unearthed.

3

FORT HILL

OYSTER BAY, NEW YORK

*F*ort Hill at Oyster Bay was one of the earliest and most strategic of all the established posts of the British on the northern shore of Long Island. It was also a very successful model of British defense planning during the Revolutionary War. There is significant historical information about the village at the period of the British occupation due to the recordings of a number of compelling and important individuals who resided here during the American Revolution. The records of the military establishment of Oyster Bay are recorded in Onderdonk's *Revolutionary Incidents of Queens County* and in the papers of Oliver Delancey. Brigadier General Oliver Delancey was a Loyalist officer who resided and commanded here in the early years of the war. The post was also well documented in the Journals of Lieutenant Colonel John Graves Simcoe, who was the commander present in 1778. He achieved significant fame through the establishment and leadership of the Queens Rangers during the war. Simcoe recorded a detailed plan of the fortifications at Oyster Bay, and this cartographical drawing is invaluable for the understanding of the military post and its layout. This map may be one of the most useful drawings ever made in portraying the full system of defenses required in preparing a winter cantonment for use by the British army.

There is some controversy over the builder of the fortifications at Oyster Bay, and their exact date of construction is uncertain. We do not know if Oliver Delancey or John Simcoe was responsible for its design and construction. The first records of a unit at the post during the Revolution

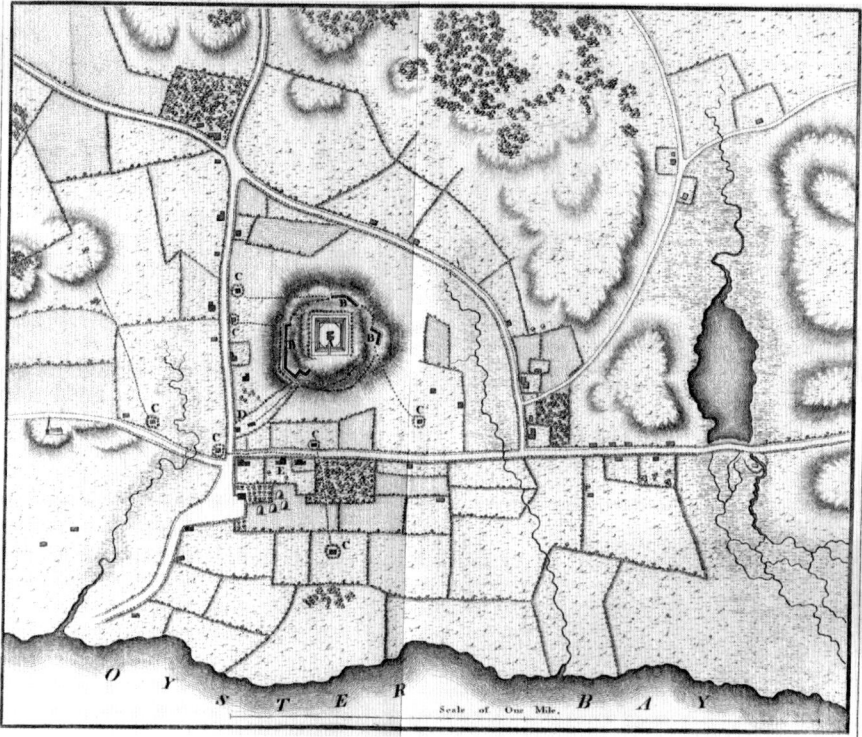

Plan of Oyster Bay, as fortified by the Queen's Rangers, by John Graves Simcoe, 1787.
Courtesy of the Norman B. Leventhal Map Center at the Boston Public Library.

are that of the forces of Oliver Delancey's Provincial Corps in either 1776 or 1777. Following that there is record of a detachment of the King's American Regiment being present in Oyster Bay under the command of Major Grant in the years 1777–78. Simcoe's regiment is recorded as arriving in November 1778 for winter quartering. In all probability, it was either in the period of residence of the Delancey Corps or that of the King's American Regiment that some or part of the fortifications was built.[43]

Histories of the post at Oyster Bay indicate that its defenses were well planned, the water source was excellent and there was plenty of food and supplies available. Troop training and exercises seemed to take up considerable amounts of the forces' time. The position of the post also allowed the army to keep a watchful eye on the north shore landing places along the Long Island Sound and Oyster Bay, which became a collection station for forage and supplies moving east–west along the length of the island.[44] There are no records that the fort and post were ever attacked by the enemy.

The most informative description of the fortifications at Fort Hill was in Simcoe's journal:

> *There was a centrical hill, which totally commanded the village, and seemed well adapted for a place of arms; the outer circuit of this hill, in the most accessible places, was to be fortified by sunken fleches, joined by abatis, and would have contained the whole corps; the summit was covered with a square redoubt, and was capable of holding seventy men; platforms were erected, in each angle, for the field pieces, and the guardhouse, in the centre, cased and filled with sand, was rendered musket proof, and looped so as to command the platforms and surface of the parapet; the ordinary guard, twenty men, were sufficient for its defence.*[45]

Simcoe's Queen's Rangers returned a few times to occupy the village of Oyster Bay after its first winter there. The description above and the unit's history are inconclusive as to whether the works were constructed in whole or in part by Simcoe's forces.

In an analysis by Peter Van Santvoord in the *Long Island Forum* in 1964, he concurs that the physical work was in all likelihood an earthwork redoubt. At each corner was a wooden platform with a field piece cannon. He also asserts that the guardhouse inside the redoubt was probably higher than the redoubt walls, of heavy wooden construction and banked with earth and stone. He continues to add that the redoubt was surrounded by an outer layer of defenses consisting of abbatis and flèches. He speculates that the flèches probably were sharpened poles set in a trench with the points angled out—the most effective defense for a cavalry attack.[46]

The famed Raynham Hall, home of Samuel Townsend, became Colonel Simcoe's headquarters and was frequented by many of the upper officers of the British army. It is also recorded that the Baptist meetinghouse was used as a barracks and the troops were not billeted. Onderdonk also writes that the New Light Meeting House was moved near the beach and housed the Highland and Grenadier troops. Another building, the Friends' meetinghouse, was also used as a commissary (supply) store.[47]

As for other troops, Stephenson's Light Company and Shank's Line Infantry were posted on the right side of the village. Kerr's and McCrae's companies were posted on the right flank of the redoubt in the east and south directions. Agnew's and Murray's companies were at positions on

Photo of the Friends' meetinghouse that was used as a commissary store during the Revolutionary War, circa 1870. *Courtesy of the private collection of John Hammond, Oyster Bay, New York.*

the right and left of the main flèche and facing the village. The hussars were posted between Dunlop's and Saunders's positions. Smyth's company occupied a position roughly between Saunders's position and that of Agnew and Murray.[48]

As mentioned, the Simcoe map—"Plan of Oyster Bay," drawn in 1787—remains one of the best records of the layout of the village during the Revolutionary War. The redoubt can clearly be seen at the center on the height with its guardhouse and its gun platforms. The gun platforms can be seen at the fort's corners. It shows the typical plan layout of a regular square redoubt work with a parapet, ditch and abbatis surrounding it on all sides. Outside of this are the series of flanking flèches, or *redans*, linked with the abbatis. These outworks look like they were set about halfway down the hill from the top of the height.

In an overlay by this author of the Simcoe map on a present-day aerial photo by Google Earth, we are able to confirm that the redoubt in the map is set at the highest point of today's Fort Hill—near the present intersection of Orchard and Simcoe Streets. A measurement of the redoubt dimensions on the aerial in actual scale indicate that it was approximately one hundred feet by one hundred feet. In the Peter Van Santvoord analysis mentioned earlier it is written that the Oyster Bay fort was thought to be similar in size to Fort Slongo, which was said to have been fifty feet square.[49] This author's analysis hints that the redoubt may actually have been much larger—almost double the size of Fort Slongo. These larger dimensions would make sense, as the corner cannon placements would have required a larger dimension for the overall redoubt.

Measuring the guardhouse at the fort's center in a similar way reveals its greatest width and depth were approximately forty feet by forty feet. Today, the rubble remains of a stone well near the crown of the hill can still be seen in a private backyard. It is unclear as to whether it existed at the time of the Revolutionary War. Reviewing the map overlay, if the well existed in the period, its approximate location would have set it just inside the flèches and abbatis outwork on the hill. The period map shows no description or markings of a well at the position.

The entrance to the redoubt can be seen in the Simcoe drawing at the center of the north side of the fort. This is inconsistent with fortification theories, as this would have positioned the entrance in what would have been considered the enemy front or the Long Island Sound side. The map also shows an abbatis flanking what appears to be a passage from the main north–south road up unto the hill of the redoubt. The building adjacent to the road at the entry to the passage is noted on the map as the "Quarters of the Huzzars," which would have been the main cavalry position. This may have been the access point from the main road up to and into the defended way up to the entry of the redoubt.

In the previous chapter, the idea of outposts or advanced posts was discussed, and the direction taken from the engineering principles of the

View up Prospect Street towards Fort Hill today, Oyster Bay, New York. *Photo by the author.*

Panorama view of the intersection of Prospect and Simcoe Streets today, Oyster Bay, New York. *Photo by the author.*

time was that any advanced posts should be flanking one another and set up approximately 200 paces apart.[50] The Simcoe map shows a number of positions labeled as "Quarters separately fortified." The positions do flank one another and do somewhat encircle the fortified hill of the redoubt. Taking a measurement on the overlay analysis by the author, the positions do range from approximately 150 paces to 225 paces apart from one another. The plan does show a building and abbatis at each of these advanced stations. These may have been positions with independent standalone blockhouses, possibly surrounded by ditches and abbatis.

Today, there are no recognizable traces of the former fortifications at the intersection of Orchard and Simcoe Streets. The area was developed as a private residential neighborhood long ago. There is nothing aside from the height of the land that hints at the historical significance of the site. It does seem that the remains of earthworks were alluded to by earlier authors in the nineteenth century. Today, nothing in the way of preservation of this site has been passed down—except for a small cemetery plot at the edge of the height in the location of the Fort Hill Burying Ground. Unfortunately, Fort Hill's location in Oyster Bay was at the center of the village, and through the growth of this area, residential development enveloped the site.

It is very fortunate that we have a discernable period map of this important post in Oyster Bay from the Revolutionary War period. Simcoe's map makes it clear that the central redoubt and its outworks were designed in accordance with other British posts of the region and for the most part

46

followed period rules for their design. The map also helps us understand the fortifications within the the larger context of the village, giving us insight into a diverse network of advanced positions and paths leading into and out of the settlement and fort. The defensive layers hint at the action of dominating the landscape, giving insight into the defenses required to maintain and defend an occupied and populated position. With the preservation of the Simcoe map, we are able to study and learn much more about the period and site than we would with only archaeological remains and written records.

4

FORT FRANKLIN

LLOYD HARBOR, NEW YORK

*F*ort Franklin was the largest British fortification on Long Island during the Revolutionary period and saw the most action of all the island's forts. It also has the honor of being the best preserved of all the fortifications covered within this book.

The site was on a prominence of land on the west side of Lloyd's Neck and had a commanding view of the entrance to Oyster Bay and Cold Spring Harbor. Lloyd's Neck was an oddly shaped peninsula that projected out into the Long Island Sound. It had only a causeway to grant access to the neck, and during high tide, it was rendered effectively an island. The fort itself was first established as a woodcutters' camp in 1777—supplying British troops primarily in Brooklyn and Manhattan with needed fuel—and also served as a refugee camp for Loyalists from the Connecticut mainland. Also at this time, a works was established to protect the woodcutters and refugees from raids by Rebels that were initiated from the Connecticut shore. In the *Long Island Forum*, Andrus Valentine discussed the fort's output: "The wood being cut for the King's Troops, nearly 2000 cords, was mostly from exceedingly large trees, some growing 40 or 50 feet before a branch put out."[51]

After 1778–79, the camp was under the command of Lieutenant Colonel Simcoe of the Queen's Rangers of Oyster Bay. He ordered that the earlier works—which were small and square—were to be strengthened with pickets set into its sides and two guns placed overlooking the harbor. Two additional guns were mounted on the east side of the works.[52] By 1779, the additionally needed fortifying had come under the supervision of Lieutenant Colonel

Richard Hewlett and were completed by Conklin's militia company. A large parade ground was created on the east side of the fort and extended for about a half a mile. This ensured a clear field of fire from the fort's ramparts.[53] At that time, a 130-foot-deep well was dug on the outskirts of the fort.[54] By 1780, Sir Henry Clinton, the British commander in New York City, had commissioned a unit called the Associated Loyalists. The unit was made up of combined Tory militia and privateer compatriots and was raised primarily to aid in countering rebel efforts against Long Island. The fort became the unit's primary headquarters. The fort's name was also changed at this time to Fort Franklin in honor of William Franklin—a former royal governor of New Jersey and the son of Patriot Benjamin Franklin. He was the newly appointed president of the Honorable Board of Associated Loyalists.[55] There is also claim that the fort was designed by Benjamin Thompson, who was also the builder of Fort Golgotha in Huntington later in the war. Thompson was to gain scientific fame later in his life. It is unknown when he might have been involved in the design or building of Fort Franklin.[56]

In early histories of the fort, we are able to find clear descriptions of its layout and specific details of its construction. One of the best descriptions is from a recorded rebel spy, a Dr. Potter:

> *The Fort on Lloyd's Neck is an irregular square, has a fosse 4 ft deep and wide, nearly surrounding it; frized on every part, upright pickets 8 ft high and 4 in diameter, (mostly of round saddlewood) are placed in the centre of the ditch and another row of pickets without the ditch, and an abbatis without the whole. A wagon passage opens into the fort, and is not obstructed by a gate. Near the centre of the fort is a block house of 4 in plank without loopholes. On the walls of the fort are mounted 4 long 12 pounders and two 3 pounders and in the fort a 4 pound field piece.*[57]

Equally compelling is an early map supposedly supplied to Benjamin Tallmadge by Abraham Woodhull in 1780. It shows the irregular layout of the fortification but has the entry to the fort in the southwest corner. It does highlight the areas of pickets, abbatis and blockhouse similar to the description by the presumed Dr. Potter.

In a beautifully illustrated map of the period by an anonymous source and its referenced legend, we can see specific notes regarding the fortification at the time. "A double block house, Magazine for 60 Barrels of Powder & Provision Store. Mounting 1 Four Pounder for the Defense of the Harbour, with a wall Stockaded, Ditch and Double Abbatis in good

Plan of Fort Franklin, August 1780. Believed to be by Abraham Woodhull to Benjamin Tallmadge. *Library of Congress.*

repair." The marking of some sort of artillery platform at its southeast corner can be clearly seen within the illustration.[58]

As previously mentioned, the fortification was a significant base of operations for the British on Long Island. In 1779, it was the Rebel whaleboat fleet that initiated its first attack on the fort. It is recorded that on September 15, 1779, Benjamin Tallmadge reached the woodcutters' camp with 130 of his dismounted light dragoons, attacked about 500 Tories and captured most of them before returning to Connecticut. There is no mention of an attempt to take the fort.[59]

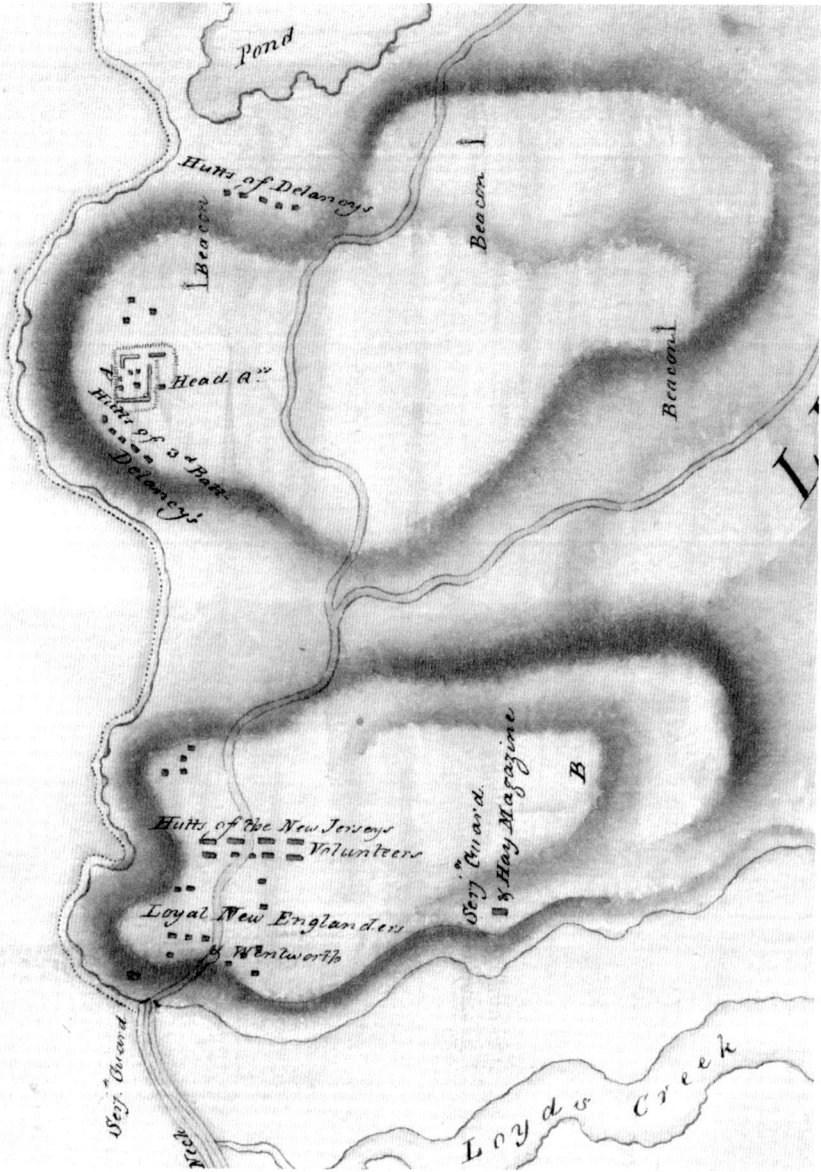

"A sketch of Lloyd's Neck. Particularly shewing the situation of the redoubt, encampment of the troops, with the ground adjacent and position of the advanc'd picket's." *Courtesy of the William L. Clements Library, the University of Michigan, Ann Arbor, Michigan.*

In 1781, another larger rebel force from Connecticut had set its course for attacking Fort Franklin. The attack force landed its troops on the unguarded beaches of the northern shore of Lloyd's Neck on July 12, 1781. In columns, the infantry moved toward the fort through the woods with a Lieutenant Heathcote Muirson directing the route and acting as a guide. He had scouted the enemy works just days before.

The force headed through the woods for another mile, attempting its attack on the eastern side of the fort. This was believed to have been the undefended side of the fort—without any heavy artillery cannon in place. The American force halted at the timberline at the east of the parade ground and formed into line formation for the attack.

The left flank of the Loyalist line was led by Lieutenant Colonel Hubbel's Regiment of Loyal Refugees. The center of the line included some of Colonel Robinson's Loyal American Regiment, Colonel Chalmer's Maryland Loyalists, the Second Battalion of New Jersey Volunteers, Colonel Wentworth's New Hampshire Volunteers, Captain Frost's Company of New England Volunteers, Captain Ives's Company of Associated Refugees and a detachment of Colonel Ludlow's Third Battalion of General DeLancey's Loyalist Brigade. The right flank was probably held by Lieutenant Colonel Pattinson's Battalion of the Prince of Wales Regiment. The total number of Loyalist troops in the line was between six hundred and seven hundred men.[60]

The American line was commanded by Major Benjamin Tallmadge of the Continental Dragoons. Tallmadge's allied force marched out onto the parade ground and halted roughly four hundred yards from the fort's eastern wall. The line was made up of Major Tallmadge's dismounted Second Continental Dragoons on the right; Patriots of the Huntington Militia, Suffolk County Refugees, Queens County Refugees and a number of Connecticut Volunteers in the center; and the French Battalion on the left flank. Altogether, the total force numbered around 450 men.[61]

Both sides advanced in line formation across the parade ground until they were within effective musket range. They then halted when 150 yards apart. The officers commanded their lines to fire controlled volleys at the enemy. As the confrontation waged on, it became clear that the Loyalist militia was not going to be routed or captured by the inferior American force. The Americans changed their tack and planned to attack and destroy the unprotected huts of the enemy on the south side of the fort.

Lieutenant Muirson, the American guide, was sent to the American left flank to scout the enemy and lead the French forces toward the Loyalist camp. The force had to march uphill to a height across two hundred yards of open ground to make the attack. The attack was perceived by the Loyalists to be an attempt to place artillery on the southern exposure and thus allow a field of fire into the fort. At this time, the Loyalists came into position on the east wall of the fort and loaded up the twelve-pounder cannon to cover the open ground with fire outside the fort. After the first discharge (and to the surprise of the uninformed Americans), the unsuspected cannons on this eastern front hushed the battlefield and the attacking force.

Following this, the fort's guns commenced in a continuous cannonade of grapeshot against the French attack force to its southeast. French soldiers fell wounded and writhing in their desperate attack on this side of the fort. The defense became too much for the attacking forces, and they retired eastward to the woods outside of the plain and there set up a field hospital for aiding the wounded.[62]

It became clear that the allied forces were outnumbered and lacked artillery support; their only choice was to retreat. Major Tallmadge's columns disappeared from the battlefield and retreated back to the beach under the protection of a rear guard.[63] Thus ended the actions at the fort. It was maintained as a Loyalist post and camp for refugees to the end of the war. It is recorded as having been the largest Loyalist refugee camp in the American Revolution—eight hundred inhabitants—for a period in 1781. At the end of the war the fort and camp was abandoned and most of its inhabitants returned to England and other Loyalist-granted lands.[64]

The fort's more modern history is equally compelling. It is safe to say that by the mid- to late nineteenth century there was enough of the remains of Fort Franklin visible and preserved in rather good order that the ruins demonstrated the fort's historical importance within its period. It was at this time that the fort evolved into its second stage of existence as an important historical artifact, and it drew the particular interest of many of its contemporaries. In 1879, Anne Alden purchased the property and had a Shingle-style house designed by Charles McKim of McKim, Mead & Bigelow (later McKim, Mead & White) built in the western portion of the former fort. Workers were reported to have unearthed a cache of relics while digging the foundation. They recovered musket balls and cannon shot and the gravestone of a Loyalist soldier in a nearby field.[65] Today, these relics exist in the mansion's garden wall in the inner courtyard of the fort's surrounding berms. This reliquary can only be presumed to have been built in the later architectural period of the twentieth century.

House for Mrs. A.C. Alden on Fort Hill, Lloyd's Neck, Long Island, 1879 architectural drawing by McKim, Mead & Bigelow. The remains of the earthworks can be seen creating a court in the foreground. *Library of Congress.*

Interestingly, the 1879 landscape design of the property integrated the earthworks of the fort into a formal circular drive and drop-off at the eastern side of the house. The roadway entered through the remains of the eastern berm and ringed the southeast corner of the earthwork to finish at a porte-cochere at the main entry of the house. An early architectural exterior rendering and floor plan shows the earthwork berms integrated into this eastern side of the main house. Also of interest is a note given in an address by the Reverend Woolsey on the Lloyd Manor of Queens Village in 1925. He referenced Fort Franklin and the then Fort Hill House: "Remains of the fort are preserved not only in the earth-works, but also in the palisade extending across the face of the cliff, built of upstanding locust logs, now enclosed and protected by a facing of concrete, which also supports the esplanade above, a passage being left behind the concrete wall."[66]

Members of the Alden family sold the home in 1900 to William John Matheson, a wealthy chemist and businessman. He built a brick-and-limestone Tudor manor house over the existing structure and expanded the footprint. This structure is the house that exists on the property today. The Tudor house built in this period further destroyed the berm wall of the earthwork. In the construction of a new entry wing running east–west and perpendicular to the main house, the southern portion and a small part of the eastern earthworks were removed. The new wing allowed access to an interior court via a newly created porte-cochere. This entry allowed an exterior court space to evolve within the historical center of the old fort's berms.

Detail looking toward the porte-cochere with the berm of the former parapet wall on the left, Fort Hill, Lloyd's Neck, Lloyd Harbor. *Library of Congress.*

Matheson's daughter, Ann Matheson Wood, inherited the house, and after her death, her will turned the property over to a foundation tasked with giving the place to a nonprofit. The Fort Hill Foundation was established but proved difficult to maintain. The foundation tried to sell the property to another nonprofit in hopes that the property could be preserved and kept up. The property was also listed in the National Register of Historic Places at this time.

In the early 1990s, private owners Greg and Kimberly Campbell were able to purchase the property and put considerable effort and expense into restoring and maintaining the property and gardens. *Newsday*, a local Long Island paper, reported in the 1990s, "They had to cut into the berms during the house restoration and had to replace the areas with clean fill."[67]

It is interesting to consider that this rebirth of the fort and its evolution into a landscaping element of a contemporary house could have been well received in its day. It may ultimately have seemed improper or apathetic in respect to its former historical glory. In retrospect, it should be indisputable that the integration of this fort into this nineteenth-century piece did ensure its preservation into the present day.

The author has spent considerable time reviewing the remains of the site. The earthworks can be clearly seen on the north and east sides of the old Tudor house. The open plain and historic well are all in the proximity of the old fort's eastern exposure. Through an analysis via aerial imagery of the earthworks and a cross-reference of the early architectural drawings of the 1879 house, the existing earthwork rectangle can be measured to be about 150 feet by 125 feet in size. This would classify the fort as a large work and irregular in its rectangular layout. All of the fort's apparent characteristics and early histories would correlate—at least in the author's mind—with other redoubt forms, making it not atypical of other British forms of posts on Long Island.

The berms are approximately four and a half feet tall, and their front and back slopes are at about a forty-five-degree angle in relation to their grade. There is no slope ascertained at the top of the earthwork, which would give evidence for the use of a *plunge* construct.[68] The slight slope of the top of the parapet would have provided a level shelf for the defenders to aid them in firing down and into their attackers.

In regards to the existing berm, if we are to take into account the theories of Lochee's book *Elements of Fortifications*, the existing berm/parapet walls would not meet the minimum dimensions for such constructions. The minimum suggested height was six feet. However, this does not take into account the historical height of the modern grade in relation to the level of the historical fort. Further archaeological analysis would need to be made to confirm this.

Panorama view of the earthwork remains today with the parade ground to the west and the well in the extreme left of the photo, Fort Hill, Lloyd's Neck, New York. *Photo by the author.*

The existing site also lacks any evidence of the ditch that would have surrounded the parapet embankments. Its historical dimensions would have been in relation to the ruins of the parapet. In this regard, we can only assume that the ditch was between four and a half feet deep to six feet deep. This would have extended the dimensions of the fort another number of feet beyond the footprint of the present berms. Beyond that would be the historically noted abbatis, thus expanding the coverage of the fort and creating its initial line of defense.

Accordingly, the entrance to the fort in relation to Lochee's writings would set a preference for it to be set "in the side or face least exposed."[69] This would support evidence for the accuracy of the presumed spy map, which sets the main fort entrance at the southwest corner of the rectangular work and out of the direct lines of attack from the east and west sides.

It is unclear where the guns and parapet embrasures would have been made in the fort's embankments. Later writings from 1923 record that there were four long twelve-pounders and two three-pounder cannons mounted on the walls and that a brass four-pound field piece was inside the fort.[70] Except for the previous note regarding the graphic in the 1780 map denoting a gun platform, no other locations of cannons can be determined.

The 1780 map of the the neck aids significantly in demonstrating the distribution of the forces in the specific area of the fort and demonstrates its importance as a center of operations. Due to the population of Loyalist forces and any number of unknown refugees who lived within the complex, its influence cannot be underestimated. The 1780 map also makes note of a number of beacons in the area and calls attention to a site of other important commanding ground in case further fortifications were needed. All these descriptions further reinforce the idea that Fort Franklin and its location on the neck were of primal importance to the British and Loyalist causes of the area.

5

EAST FORT

LLOYD HARBOR, NEW YORK

*T*he east end of Lloyd's Neck was the location of another fort and advanced position that worked in association with Fort Franklin at the time. It is also referred to and recorded as the East Fort. The eastern end of Lloyd's Neck was also known for a large erratic boulder called Target Rock sitting at the shoreline. The rock was known to have been a target for cannon practice by British warships during the Revolutionary War. Initially, the East Fort site was recorded as an advanced post on the eastern approach to Fort Franklin and a guard position guarding the Huntington Harbor approach by water. At some point, this post became a shore battery, and an earthwork was constructed there. It is described as having two twelve-pounder cannons that were taken from the decks of British warships in 1781.[71] A period map of Lloyd's Neck also labels the eastern position on a height "Advanced Picket of a Sub(Subaltern Officer) and 20 Private." The drawing is presumed to be from 1780.[72] There aren't any records stating what troops were stationed at this post, but it can be assumed they were members of the combined forces garrisoning Fort Franklin.

In Onderdonk's book *Revolutionary Incidents in Queens County* is a sketch of the attack on Lloyd's Neck in 1781. He labeled the eastern portion of the map with a description: "Probable place where the British armed schooner landed her guns and mounted them in a battery on shore, and so beat off a 40 gun ship that came to the attack."[73] Other coastal maps made in the 1830s clearly show the outlines of an irregular fort on a height of land that appears to jut out slightly into the bay along the shoreline along the cliffs.

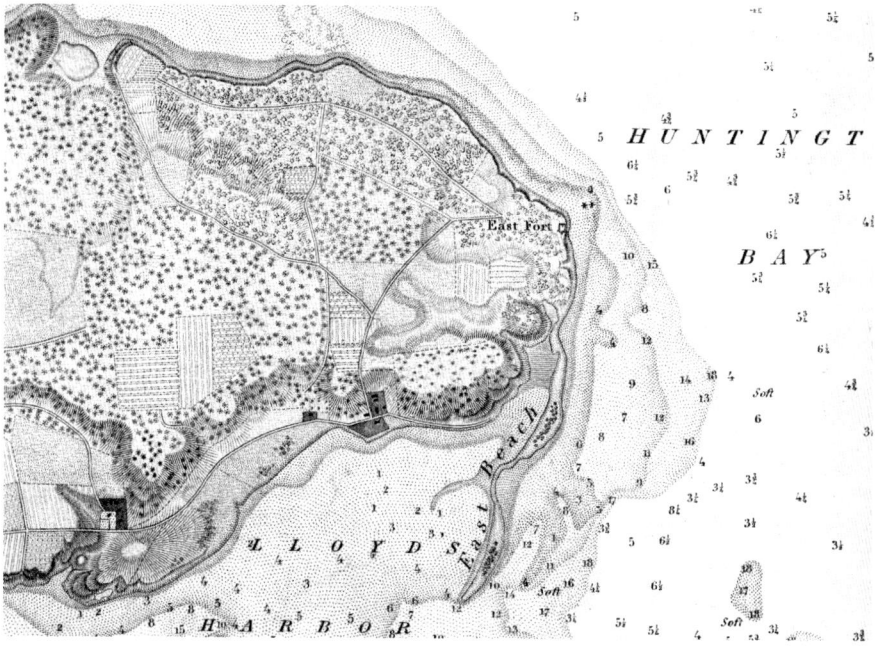

Above: Section of Huntington Bay Map. Survey under the direction of F.R. Hassler, 1849. The East Fort is marked on the east shore of Lloyd's Neck. *Courtesy of the David Rumsey Historical Map Collection.*

Opposite, top: An early map showing the East Fort and the terrain around it. From a map of Cold Spring and Oyster Bay Harbors, North Shore of Long Island, 1836. *Courtesy of the University Libraries Digital Research Collections, Stony Brook University.*

Opposite, bottom: Vintage photo of Target Rock, shoreline and cliffs, 1905. From an early postcard of Lloyd's Neck, Long Island. *Author's collection.*

Further records or details about the post at this position are lacking. There is little history written about it, even in the descriptions of Fort Franklin. Local historical societies in the area know little about its existence.

The area where this fortification would have been was later located on an eighty-acre estate called the Target Rock Farm. This was an estate site established in the early twentieth century by Rudolph Flinsch. In 1936, the property was sold to investment banker Ferdinand Eberstadt, who had a Georgian-style mansion with magnificent gardens designed and built by architects Delano and Aldrich in 1937–38. In 1967, Eberstadt donated the property to the federal government.[74] The site of the fort is now within the boundaries of the Target Rock National Wildlife Refuge, which is an eighty-acre preserve and park. The coastal maps showed that the fortification was

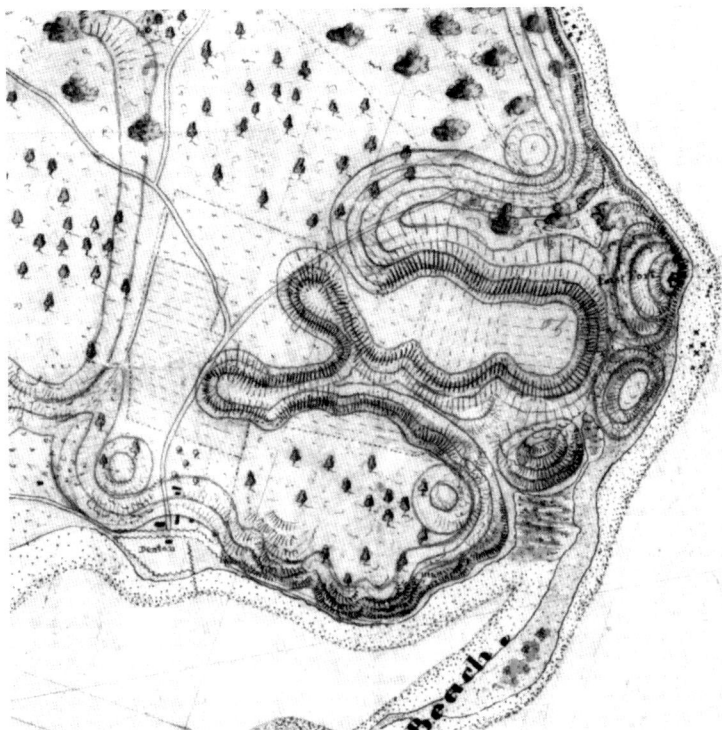

A similar view of Target Rock and shoreline today, Lloyd's Neck, New York. *Photo by the author.*

located close to Target Rock. An observation of the presumed area of the fort by this author affirms that neither a height nor a projection of land exists today along the cliffs. The cliff is relatively straight and parallel to the beach, but it has been severely damaged due to erosion. In a 1923 issue of the *Long Islander* newspaper, a reporter states that the fort on the east side of Lloyd's Neck had since disappeared by erosion into Huntington Harbor. Another description of the area recorded that the Target Rock was set into the side of the cliff during the time of the American Revolution. A vintage photograph from 1905 shows the rock separated from the cliff. A modern photo in the same direction shows the cliff has receded much more from the location of the boulder seen in the vintage 1905 photo.

The coastal maps of the early 1830s may be the only clues to what the fort at this location would have looked like. One of the plans shows a square redoubt with a bastion at the south end. Guns for the defense of the height would have had to have been mounted pointing out toward the water to the east. It would seem that a bastion as figured in the 1930 map would assume that the guns were mounted on this bastion pointing south. This configuration would not have been to the advantage of the fort and is probably not an accurate representation of the position's layout. Another more elaborate coastal map shows the fort on the height, and it is represented as more of an oblong shape. This may have been a much closer representation of what may have existed there. Its layout seems to suit the oblong contours that defined the height more. This fort might have been merely a gun battery as its recorded history suggests with only earthen walls and not a multisided standalone redoubt like other sites on Long Island. The sketches give no hint of a blockhouse or structure existing at the position at the time.

A digital overlay of the older maps mentioned earlier with a modern aerial of the site places the positions of the extended point of land and possible fortifications over the present location of the beach and much farther out into the bay than the line of the present cliff. It is this author's belief that the earlier mentioned report of the site having eroded into the Long Island Sound is, in fact, true. The fort's destruction may have taken place in the early part of the last century and possibly between 1905—the year of the vintage photo—and 1923, the year the *Long Islander* article was printed. The East Fort's natural loss is much in sync with its place in history. Its possible existence will continue to be challenged by a lack of any form of tangibility.

6

Fort Golgotha

Huntington, New York

The village of Huntington was an important location along the northern shore of Long Island during the Revolutionary War. The volume of records describing the stay of many British troop units and high command personalities between the years 1775 and 1783 attests to the importance of the village. The British maintained their largest number of posts and fortifications in this general area. Huntington was also close to the important Fort Franklin headquarters on Lloyd's Neck.

There were other earlier fortifications established in the town, but in 1782, it became the desire of an American-born Loyalist named Benjamin Thompson to create a fort on the consecrated hilltop of the town's burying ground. Thompson, who was formerly a member of Lord North's cabinet in London, had managed to get a commission as a colonel of cavalry and came to Huntington as the commander of the King's Dragoon Regiment. Later in life, Thompson became Count Rumford, a minister of war and police in Bavaria.[75]

In November 1782, late in the Revolutionary War, Thompson desecrated the holy ground of the burying ground, leveling many of the graves at the top of the hill in the old cemetery east of Main Street. He ordered a fort and a field kitchen—called Fort Golgotha after the biblical "Place of the Skull"—to be erected there at the graveyard's summit. While building the fort, his troops destroyed over one hundred tombstones, cut down 114 apple and pear trees, stripped 390 feet of boards from local barns and destroyed the local Presbyterian church, taking 1,000 feet of boards from

Panorama view of the Old Burying Ground today. The photo is looking west parallel with the elongated height that was formerly the site of Fort Golgotha, Huntington, New York. *Photo by the author.*

a nearby meetinghouse. Tombstones served as tables and were used for building fireplaces and ovens. The local inhabitants saw loaves of bread being eaten by the British with the reversed inscriptions of the tombstones imprinted on the crust. The fort was erected in fifteen days by pressed laborers and carpenters.[76]

The Huntington Town Records state that the fort's front faced north toward the harbor and gave the following description of its layout:

> *It is about 5 rods in front with a gate in the middle, it extends a considerable distance north and south; the works were altogether of earth, about six foot high, no pickets or any other obstruction to the works, except a sort of ditch, which was very inconsiderable some brush like small trees fixed on the top of the works in a perpendicular form.*[77]

Adding to this description it also states that the the troops were quartered as compactly as possible in the inhabitants' houses and barns, and some hutted along the sides of the fort. These barracks were recorded as places of revelry, profanity and debauchery, all adding to the desecration of the historical burying ground, the sacred resting place of the local inhabitants of the last one hundred years. The forces recorded as being present at the fort were the men of Thompson's dragoon regiment, troops of the Queen's Rangers and members of the British Legion under Tarleton. The forces consisted of 550 men.[78]

It is also recorded that some gravestones also served as doorsteps for the fort. Among the graves that were desecrated was that of Reverend Ebenezer

Prime, who was the minister of the Presbyterian church from 1723 until his death in 1779. He was an enthusiastic supporter of the American Revolution and the Rebel cause. It is reported that when the fort was built, Colonel Thompson made sure that its exit was placed in front of the Reverend Prime's grave so that he would have the pleasure of "treading on the old Rebel" whenever he departed or entered the fort.[79]

There are no records that the fort was ever attacked while in existence. By November 3, 1783, the war had ended, and the British and Loyalist forces left Huntington. The fort was then destroyed by the local inhabitants, and an auction was held to dispose of materials that could be salvaged from it. The burial ground once again became the resting place of future generations of Huntington inhabitants, and the gravestones again covered the summit position that was the fort.[80] Today, there are some recognizable earthwork remains left. Although they are low-lying berms, they do give us some insight into the position of the fort at the time.

Today, the graveyard exhibits a long, level plain at the most extreme height of the site. An analysis by this author has recorded the approximate length and width of the flat rectangular area of the cemetery at its height. The rectangular area is approximately 130 feet long by 50 feet wide. Some of the edges of this flat area fall away to become the slopes of the graveyard mount, giving an irregular edge to this plateau at the top. At the extreme south of the position there are two slight berm corners forming what may be the southern parapet walls of the fort. Through a study of aerial photos of the site, the author has observed that from these berms can be seen the north–south edges along the plateau. These may be the lines of the parapet walls and ditch.

There is an old sketch plan done by an earlier author presumed to be a representation of Fort Golgotha. It states that it was deducted from details given in a spy report. It shows an irregular rectangular layout that was wider at the extreme south and narrower at the north and showed bastions at each of its four corners. As the previous paragraph mentioned, the ruined earthworks at the site today show the southern corners and long north–south walls to be relatively parallel to one another. There are no signs that bastions would have existed at the fort's corners. Also, there are no period examples or references that would support this type of redoubt configuration.

This author has developed a conjectural plan layout based on the analysis of the site, and it has been constructed making some assumptions based on period notes and references. The historical recorded dimension of the front of the fort was five rods, which is approximately 82 feet today. Of course, we

Slope

Grave of
Ebenezer Prime

To Harbor
North

Entry

Ditch

Ditch

Gate

Ditch

Abattis at
Parapet

Slope

Barracks

Slope

Ditch

Ditch

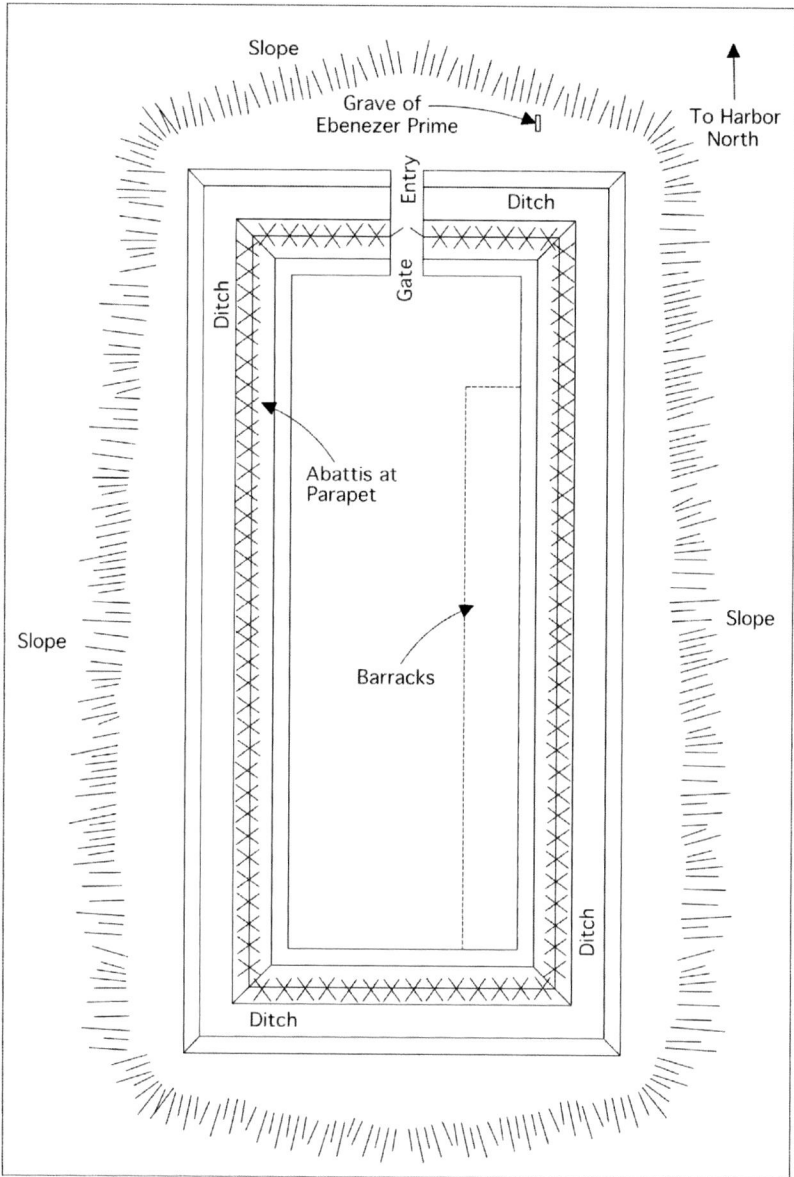

Conjectural plan layout of Fort Golgotha in the years 1782–83. *Drawing by the author.*

do not have any way of confirming the exact points or positions that these dimensions referred to, but it is interesting to make a comparison based on some recorded dimensions taken from the site today. If we take into account the 50-foot width based on the berms and add the approximated width of a ditch to both sides we would come to an approximate overall width in the range of 75 to 85 feet on this northern side. Likewise, its north–south dimension would be around 150 to 160 feet. This author speculates that the fort was an elongated redoubt much in accordance with historical records. A redoubt of this form differed greatly from the more typical layout of other fort sites on Long Island. It seems that the work here was situated much in sync with the natural landscape. Its construction methods, individual features and materials would have been much in common to other posts on Long Island.

The gravestone of Ebenezar Prime can still be seen just north of the flat portion at the hilltop at the point that the slope of the hill descends. If the gate was truly at the north—opening toward the harbor and set in the center of the fort on the side on entering the gate from the east—Thompson may

A close-up view today of the old gravestone of Ebenezer Prime in the Old Burying Ground, Huntington, New York. *Photo by the author.*

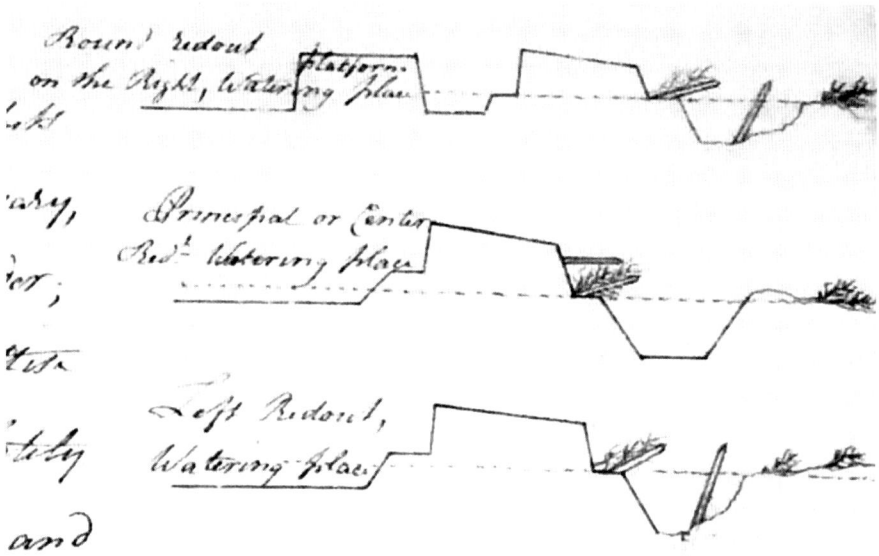

Cross-sections of six redoubts on Staten Island from assistant engineer Lieutenant George Sproule's report, December 9, 1780. *Courtesy of the William L. Clements Library, the University of Michigan, Ann Arbor, Michigan.*

have, in fact, had to pass over the grave of the Reverend Prime. There is only some truth to this, presuming the grave marking is in its authentic and original location. This present location has aided the author in calculating the possible position of the northern wall of the fort.

One of the more interesting and unique elements recorded in the description of the fort noted in the Huntington Town Records was that there were some "brush like small trees fixed on the top of the works in a perpendicular form."[81] Although the typical redoubt would have been composed of horizontal fascines (sharpened horizontal stakes) at the parapet wall, the description seems to note a brush-like construction at the wall. This type of fascine construction may be more similar to period construction principles than we think. Period sketches of many British redoubts on Staten Island drawn in cross-section seem to show that some of the works there employed horizontal stakes that were covered by an abbatis. These sketches confirm that this was possibly the defensive wall configuration used at Fort Golgotha.

The barracks, which were described as some sort of lean-to, may have been a last-minute structure set up due to a limited availability of lumber.

As it was late in the war and the British likely saw the post as a temporary construct, this barracks may have been a rudimentary form of short-term housing for troops. It seems very unlikely that this would have been outside of the parapet wall and in the ditch. That placement would really undermine the notion or need for the fortification. The parapet wall probably acted as one side of the barrack structure on the inside of the fort—reducing the need for greater construction material.

Fort Golgotha is historically remembered as a detested violation of the burial grounds of early Huntington's inhabitants by the enemy. The construction occurred late in the Revolutionary War, so its development tells us a little more about how the design of a fortification had progressed by this later period. It seems that there was a desperation and bitterness within the British commanders, and this manifested itself in the urgency of the construction and the total disregard for the local population during its execution. The works at this site also display a particular uniqueness in their design from the earlier regular works of the typical redoubt of the area. This may be a byproduct of progressed fortification evolution within the final years of the war or a natural form that developed based on the inherent characteristics of the site.

7

FORT HILL

HUNTINGTON, NEW YORK

To the east and south of the center of Huntington and on its northeastern and southwestern approaches there were other fortifications of an earlier period than that of Fort Golgotha. There was a small earthwork recorded on a height of ground near the Episcopal church northeast of the village. This is now the site of the Bethel African Methodist Episcopal Church and St. John's Cemetery on Park Avenue in Huntington.[82] To the southwest of Huntington, there were also records of visible remains existing of a defensive position at the Place Farm in West Hills that today would be near the Whitman-Place House east of West Hills Road.[83] There was yet another larger fort on a hill near a site called Gallows Hill. This site has since been called Fort Hill.

Huntington was one of the villages on Long Island that was garrisoned, fortified and occupied permanently throughout the Revolutionary War by the British. It was a central position on the North Shore of the island and became the headquarters for British foraging parties of cavalry ranging the countryside. Its many bays and inlets allowed the village to be accessible to British ships out on Long Island Sound.[84]

According to Platt's *Old Times in Huntington*, there were thousands of troops in the Huntington camp and its forts during the period. The Huntington post housed quarters for the Seventeenth Light Dragoons, Seventy-First Infantry, the British Legion of Cavalry, the Queen's Rangers, Colonel Hewlett's Provincials, the Loyal Refugees, Jersey Loyal Volunteers, the Hessian Yagers and the Prince of Wales American Regiment.[85]

Illustration of a sergeant of the British 17th Light Dragoons, 1779. *Courtesy of K/S Historical Publications and Imrie/Risley Miniatures.*

Official orders of General Delancey on July, 11, 1777, state, "The Inhabitants must be Summoned to assist in Constructing a small Redoubt at some distance in the rear of the Camp to Hold a Serjeants Guard and also to build a redoubt in the front of the Camp to retire to in case of a well grounded Alarm."[86] Although this order is not specific as to the location of the fortifications, it does give some record of there being two redoubts present in Huntington. It also asserts that General Delancey was the builder of the works.

Records show that an embankment had been established and a small fort created at the site of Fort Hill. The story of the site is remembered not so much by the British post located there but by the hangings that took place nearby at Gallows Hill. One of the early legends is that two American spies were hanged by the British on the hill close by the fort.[87]

The other recorded history is that Loyalists of Lloyd's Neck had terrorized local inhabitants by hanging them and then cutting them down just before they would pass out. This was a method of forcing local Rebels to give secret information regarding the hiding of valuables. In one instance, the Loyalists went too far, and one man died as a result.[88]

These offenders became captives of the British forces but then managed to escape. The British had sent a detachment of cavalry officers to hunt the men down, and eventually, they were found hiding in the village. The captured men were found guilty of the crimes and forced to ride to their place of execution on top of their prepared coffins by oxcart.[89]

The route of their journey to Gallows Hill was as follows:

Their course was easterly, and it continued as until they reached a steep incline, where the road seemed to have been made by the excavation of a steep hill that ran parallel with the roadbed for about a hundred yards making a perpendicular bank, shelving at the top so much as to be overhanging some portions of the road. The cart was drawn to the very top of the hill.[90]

At the site, the offenders were helped off the cart and to their coffins. With very little ceremony, they were executed.[91]

In the Oliver Delancey Papers, the guarding of the fort and orders for its defense were recorded:

> *Huntington Camp, 25th Aug 1777*
> *B:Odrs The Inutility of a Sentry at the Fort Gate & the Necessity of his being on the North Rampart is so obvious and has been so Frequently pointed out that it was by no means thought requisite to give the following order—That a Centry be placed every night on the North Rampart of the Fort that he be ordered to walk from the Center of it to 5 or 6 paces on the East Rampart—That all prisoners be kept the night through into a Tent & a Centry to be Constantly over them.*[92]

The orders seem to acknowledge a period of heightened threat from the enemy and the necessity for vigilant defense at the northern or waterfront side of the fort. This was most likely due to the recent attack and successful defense at Fort Setauket, which had happened only three days previously.

There is an 1837 Long Island coastal map of the area of Gallows Hill showing the nearby area. At the site of Fort Hill, a small redoubt square was drawn in the middle of the height of land at the intersection of the old main road and the modern Fort Hill Road. The map shows that the

A section of an early map showing Gallows Hill and Fort Hill area (Fort Hill redoubt in center). From a map of the harbor and village of Huntington, North Shore of Long Island, 1837. *Courtesy of the University Libraries Digital Research Collections, Stony Brook University.*

Present-day view looking west along Route 25A at the site of Fort Hill, Huntington, New York. *Photo by the author.*

site was a key strategic position between Huntington and the village of Centerport. The site of the historical Gallows Hill is not clearly marked but is noted, and there are two clear heights of land north of the fort location that could be this hill.

The square fortification in the map appears to be diagonally located on its site and angled so its corners are parallel with the line of the main road into Huntington. The access to the fort is shown as a small pathway from the southwest corner to a gate at the back of the fort. This would seem appropriate, as this side would be the least exposed position in a frontal attack from the sound or from the north. The position of the fort is again typical of other posts covered in this book, it being at the junction and fork of major roadways.

Henry Platt confirms that the remains of the fort at Fort Hill were still clearly visible in 1876, the time of his writings about Huntington's local history. The site of the fort seems to have been forgotten after that, and it is unclear as to what date the ruins totally vanished from the hill. Early newspapers of the twentieth century confirm that the site's name was changed to Fort Hill from Gallows Hill when the site's significance as a British outpost was determined. Today, the site is covered by single-family homes. The remains of the fort are long gone. The approach along 25A today still displays the position's defensive merits. A fort at this location would have dominated the roadway entering Huntington village.

8

FORT SLONGO

FORT SALONGA, NEW YORK

*F*arther east of Huntington and just across the border in the town of Smithtown was another redoubt fort built by the British. It also had an interesting history during the Revolutionary War years. The post was called Fort Slongo, and its name seems to have come from contractor George Slongo of Philadelphia, who built the fort for the British.[93] Like Fort Franklin on Lloyd's Neck, it was attacked by the Americans during the war.

Fort Slongo was erected on a high point of land in Smithtown that was then known as Treadwell's Neck. The fort is recorded as being an adjunct to the larger Fort Franklin on Lloyd's Neck. There appears to be no records as to the year of its construction, but it was probably built between the years 1778 and 1779, as this was the height of the British fort-building period and was roughly the same time of the construction of Fort Franklin. The fort was a few miles north of the village of Middleville and overlooked Fresh Pond. It was approximately one hundred rods from the shore, and its position had a commanding view of Long Island Sound in several directions. It was noted as not being the highest point of land in the area but definitely had the best position to see enemy movements on the water.[94] There was a sketch drawn by an American Patriot of the post, and it was given to Henry Scudder, who also was on the side of the American cause. He aided in the later attack on the fort by the Americans. This sketch, combined with a written description, explores the fort in detail:

An early map showing the height and position of the fort (left and center of the map above the Fresh Pond). From a map of Crab Meadow, North Side of Long Island, 1837. *Courtesy of the University Libraries Digital Research Collections, Stony Brook University.*

It consisted of an embankment forming a hollow square of about 50 feet, built at the head of a small ravine that sloped abruptly westward into the valley. The walls were formed by banking earth around trees growing in their natural position and round posts set in the ground. The fort had a ditch & wall about 7 feet high—on the top of the wall is a perpendicular picket and at the foot of the wall a horizontal picket.—it has occasionally from 50 to 90 men in it.[95]

The sketch also shows the gate or sally port and a blockhouse in the center. A camp area is noted as "hutts" just outside the ditch. Enclosing the fort and the camp, an abbatis acted as the outermost line of defense.[96] The fort is recorded as having had a small detachment of mounted men present for its defense against raids.

On the evening of October 2, 1781, an American force of around one hundred men under the command of Colonel Tallmadge and led by Major Lemuel Trescott were dispatched in whaleboats from Norwalk, Connecticut, to attack and capture Fort Slongo. The previous evening, a reconnaissance party led by Sergeant Elijah Churchill was sent over. The force landed at Crab Meadow and was able to scout the area and study the surveillance map to plan the place of attack. That night, late in the early hours, the British officers from the fort were partying at the local Mulford Inn in nearby Middleville. The commanding officer, Major Valanstine, was away for military matters in New York City.[97]

The force under Trescott was composed of fifty men from Captain Richards's Company of the Connecticut Line and fifty men from Captain Edgars's Dismounted Dragoons. The force landed on the shores near the fort in the early morning hours of October 3. Captain Edgars's dragoons were ordered to surprise the garrison and the works while Captain Richards's men were to surround the fort to prevent the garrison from escaping. The attack commenced at three o'clock in the morning with Lieutenant Rogers of the Second Regiment of Light Dragoons leading the attack with a few chosen men. Major Trescott and Captain Edgars's forces followed behind. When they arrived at the fort, the sentry guard fired his gun in alarm and retreated inside. He forgot to close the gate behind him.[98] According to Tallmadge's journal, there was some opposition from the defenders when the attackers entered the fort. Four of the defenders were killed, and two were wounded. Sergeant Elijah Churchill was the only man wounded on the American side. He was one of the men in the leading attack. He is remembered as the first enlisted man to receive the Badge of Military Merit, later to be the Purple Heart, for his bravery in the attack at Fort Slongo.[99]

After the capture of the fort, all stored materials were burned, and two four-pounder cannons were spiked (rendered unusable). The Americans captured two captains, one lieutenant and eighteen privates; two one-pounder cannons; and one brass one-pounder cannon.[100] The fort and buildings were burned, rendering it effectively out of action for the remainder of the war.

There are some markings of the ruins of the fort on old maps of the area from the nineteenth century. Some written records note the site as being

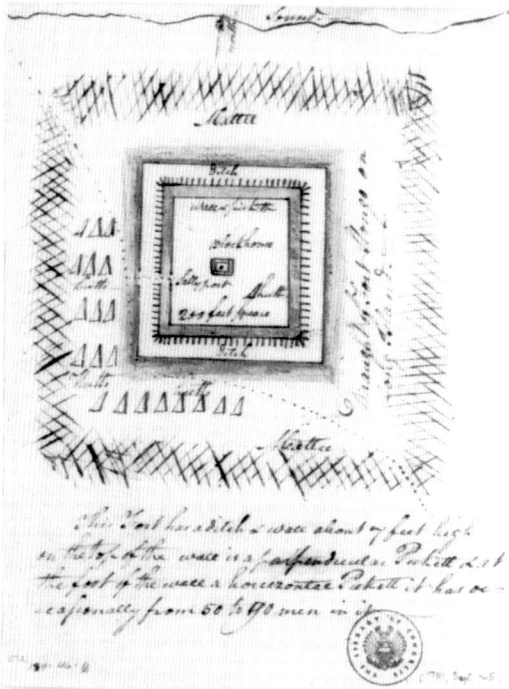

Left: Early plan sketch layout of Fort Slongo and surroundings believed to be by a Patriot spy. *Library of Congress.*

Below: View of the ruins of Fort Slongo today showing the existing top of the parapet berms and the dip at the center of the earthworks, Fort Salonga, New York. *Photo by the author.*

View of the earthworks today with the berm or parapet wall and the shallow indentation of the former ditch to the left in the photo, Fort Salonga, New York. *Photo by the author.*

passed down from owner to owner. Today, the fort is located in the backyard of a single-family home in a residential neighborhood. The houses of the neighborhood were built in the twentieth century. The fort's location in a residential neighborhood has ensured its survival into the present day.

The now-famous Scudder spy map of the fort leaves us one of the best records of a drawing of a British redoubt and its attributes in detail. It shows many similarities to other fortifications on Long Island and other redoubt principles that have been earlier discussed. One interesting difference is that the written period description on the map notes that on top of the wall there was a perpendicular picket. As the earlier chapters assert, in nearly all cases the parapet had a banquette for the troops to stand on and fire down from at any attacking force. The embankment's height and form were derived by the standard height of a man and his comfort in firing over the wall. A palisade at the top of the wall would not have facilitated this defensive scenario.

The sketch and description make it clear that the fort had horizontal fraizing along the parapet wall and above the ditch. The palisade may, in fact, have been more typical of other forts and set within and at the front of the ditch. The recording may have just been an error in observation. The perpendicular picket may also have been misinterpreted or confused with a procedure that was noted during its construction. The members were recorded as being set in the ground, and the earth was moved around them to create a more structural wall.

The ruins of the site have been analyzed and recorded by this author. The existing earthwork embankment ruins, which are about two feet tall, were paced out as approximately forty-eight to fifty feet square. The earth behind the embankment, which would have been the center of the fort, is rather high but slightly more depressed toward the center. There are dips in the ground just outside of the earthworks that would coincide with the indentations at the position of the former ditch.

It is interesting in the notes on the fort's capture that there were a number of cannons formerly employed in its defense. Most likely, the fort had its cannons set to fire over the parapet wall. This author speculates that an unknown quantity of cannons were probably set on platforms at positions in the fort. The sketch map shows a tiny blockhouse that does not seem to be feasible in its overall proportion to the size of the redoubt. In assuming the presence of cannons in the fort, it makes sense to speculate that the blockhouse was approximately ten to fifteen feet in length and width. The blockhouse probably did not employ cannon, as it would have been too small. The blockhouse, similar to that at the Oyster Bay fort, was probably used as a guardhouse and barracks for the troops. The brass field piece recorded in the fort's captured belongings might have been situated pointing internally at the fort's gate or mounted on a second level of the blockhouse. The mounting of the cannon in the blockhouse, however, would have limited its flexibility as a possible field piece outside of the fort's walls.

Fort Slongo and its ruins remain today as one of the best preserved forts on Long Island. Its remains aid in properly validating the principles of the typical regular square redoubt of the time. The ruins—combined with the documented plan from the period—are a means for truly authenticating this preserved piece from antiquity. This site has very special meaning and should be preserved for future generations.

9

FORT SETAUKET

SETAUKET, NEW YORK

*F*ort Setauket was not your typical fortification built by the British during the occupation years of the Revolution. The village of Setauket—also known as Brookhaven—was another important center for the British on the northern shore and a point of defense against rebel attacks from Connecticut. The town's Presbyterian church became the central component of the fortification in the area. Being sympathetic to the Rebel cause, the Presbyterian congregation was greatly disliked by the British command in America. Many of their places of worship were confiscated for British military use. This was the case in Setauket, and the Presbyterian church on the Setauket Common became the primary fortified position of the village. Close by and to the northwest was the Church of England. Today, this structure still exists and is known as the Caroline Church. It was maintained as a place of worship by the occupying British forces and acted as a hospital at the time of the attack on the nearby Presbyterian church. The original Caroline Church has survived until today, and its exterior has been reconstructed to represent its Revolutionary War appearance. This existing structure gives us great insight into the scale and character of a church of the period, helping us visualize the church at the time of the American Revolution.

An attack on Fort Setauket took place in the summer of 1777, so we can assume that the church was taken by the British in the early months after the American defeat at the Battle of Long Island in 1776.

The force posted at Setauket was led by Lieutenant Colonel Richard Hewlett of the Third Battalion of De Lancey's Brigade with three captains and about 260 men.[101] Records show that there was a continued presence of British troops located at Setauket. The village was on one of the major passage routes between Huntington and points farther east.

The fort at the time was described as such:

Four swivels were mounted at the galley windows and horses were stabled below. As a place of resort in case of attack, it was enclosed at a distance of 30 feet with an earthen mound 6 feet high and 5 feet thick, laid with fascines, so as to be ball proof. On top were set pickets 6 feet high and 3 inches apart. Pickets also projected from the outer side over the ditch. Two steps of earth were made inside the wall for the men to rise and fire their muskets between the pickets. A heavy double gate was on the south side.[102]

View of the east side of the present Presbyterian church and burying ground. Former site of Fort Setauket in 1777, Setauket, New York. *Photo by the author.*

An attack was organized by American forces in the summer of 1777. On August 25, 1777, General Parsons landed at Mount Misery on Long Island with five hundred men and several pieces of cannon. In the early morning hours, once in range of Fort Setauket, the American forces requested its surrender. The British forces asked for half an hour, as they were anticipating reinforcements. The Americans gave them ten minutes. The British command led by Lieutenant Colonel Hewlett consulted with his men and replied that he was determined to defend the fort to the last man.

The Americans positioned their artillery pieces near a large rock in full view of the church at a distance of three to four hundred yards from the fort. The church was recorded as being perforated from musket balls from the firing of the American attackers. The principal firing recorded from the British position was from the swivel guns. The battle had gone on for two to three hours when the Americans learned that British reinforcements were sighted on ships on the Long Island Sound. The Americans then retreated to their boats and were ferried across to Connecticut.[103]

The fort was initially recorded as being abandoned in early 1778. There are surveillance letters from Caleb Brewster attesting that Setauket was still occupied by many troops in the years 1780–81. The fortifications were probably maintained as a base throughout the entire war years. After peace, the local citizens restored the church and removed the earthworks. Some years later, the original church was struck by lightning and burned to the ground. The existing Presbyterian church on the site dates from the year 1812.[104] The original church grounds and the position of the fort have been preserved in the present site and graveyard grounds that are adjacent to the old village green. No clues to the location of the original church foundation remain. Patriot's Rock—the large boulder that the attacking Americans placed their artillery cannon near in the 1777 attack—can still be seen a little to the west of the church beside the main road. The boulder was originally a part of the village green, which was much larger at the time and included this area. The village green was treeless then and the artillery placed near the rock would have had a clear and open shot toward the enemy position at Fort Setauket. The property of Patriot's Rock is now preserved by the Three Village Community Trust and is preserved for future generations.[105]

Fort Setauket was a unique structure in that it was created by converting an existing church into a defensive fortification. Some later writings about the fort contend that much of the structure's interior was removed and the church was used as a place to keep horses during the occupation. As it would have been difficult to move horses in and out of the fort, it is more

Patriot Rock and its preserved surroundings today. Most likely the American attackers positioned their cannon on the height to the side and near the rock in 1777. This elevation would have had a clear and open view to the British fort, Setauket, New York. *Photo by the author.*

probable that the building became a guardhouse or fortified blockhouse for the troops. According to the period writings of Lewis Lochee in the *Principle of Field Fortifications*, there were distinct directions for fortifying a church or house and even for defending a churchyard. One of his principles describing fortifying of buildings was titled "To Prevent the Enemy's Forcing through the Doors or Windows." In this text, he purports that if there is a single door to the building and it is small that it is to be barricaded on the inside with planks and boards. Then there were only to be left openings or loopholes for the defenders to fire their muskets through at an attacker. Likewise, the windows of the ground floor were to be similarly boarded up and loopholes set in them. Lochee's manual even instructs that the loopholes should be set in the walls at a distance of three or four feet from one another.[106]

Beyond the building's defense, Lochee goes on to describe the outer works required in fortifying a church or house:

The defence may be much increased, by raising a curving parapet of Earth about the building, if it is isolated; and, if not so before such parts of it as are open to attack: this parapet is to be defended by as many men as can be spared, who when forced to abandon it, are to take refuge in the house.[107]

He adds that to impede the enemies' approach a ditch was to be made outside the wall but not close enough to endanger the foundation, and that when trees were at hand that they were to be laid in the ditch with their branches turned out towards the enemy.[108] This description is again very similar to the regular works of a redoubt mentioned earlier in this book, with its parapet, ditch and abbatis all set in place. Interestingly, this same defensive logic may have been utilized in fortifying the headquarters earlier mentioned at Fort Nonsense in Jericho. Both would have utilized existing buildings in a defensive manner and have been surrounded by earthworks much like a redoubt.

A plan of Brookhaven or Setalket Harbour with its environs, 1778. From a map by Samuel Holland. *Courtesy of the William L. Clements Library, the University of Michigan, Ann Arbor, Michigan.*

The Tyler-Jayne Tavern today. Recorded location of a massacre by the British during the Revolutionary War, Setauket, New York. *Photo by the author.*

The plan by Samuel Holland is an invaluable document to our understanding of the post at Setauket and clearly shows the layout of the village in 1777–78. The locations of the Presbyterian church (meetinghouse), the redoubt and the British camp to the east can be seen. The redoubt and church show the proximity of the fort to the main road and stress its importance as an essential element in the domination of this passageway. The period plan also shows that the fortified church and the adjacent camp were at an elevated point. The camp elongated along the high point of the map and was set close by and beside access to the harbor. This is similar to what can be seen in other maps of the time. It can be assumed that all of these determinations were planned by the British high command for the best defense of the forces in the immediate area.

The map also labels a location near the Mill Pond of a noted Baylies Tavern. This may be the name used at the time for the existing Tyler-Jayne Tavern of today. The building was owned by John Tyler during the Revolutionary War years. During the war, a bloody massacre took place here when British troops came looking for deserters. They opened fire on innocent people in the tavern. In the end, four Americans were found dead. Bullets from the massacre are said to still be seen in the interior of the house. It was moved from its historical position, which was farther north, to its present foundation in 1890.[109]

An analysis by the author of the site and a calculation of the possible dimensional layout of the fort in 1777 in an overlay of the existing Presbyterian church would set the measurement of the parapet earthworks to be roughly eighty by one hundred feet. As we do not know the exact dimensions of the former church, this is all speculation, and this hypothesis begins to give us an idea of the possible size of the work based on the historical recordings of the former fort's dimensions of thirty feet beyond the church walls. A physical review of the actual site does show that there is only one pre–Revolutionary War tombstone close to the present church, and it is at the back southeast corner of the existing church. The marker is approximately ten feet from the church foundations and badly damaged. This stone may have existed within the redoubt walls at the time of the fort. Also, farther to the east is a row of Satterly family tombstones that are dated prior to 1777, set parallel to the structure approximately thirty feet from the existing church's eastern wall. These graves may have existed just inside the fort walls at the time of the fort or just outside of them. As we can presume there was a ditch outside the parapet walls, it makes sense that these were most likely just inside the fort's parapet walls.

In an aerial photo analysis of the distance between Patriot's Rock and the fort, it can be determined that they were approximately 260 yards apart. Historically, this is recorded as being 300 to 400 yards from the fort. The Holland map also marks the location of a position of commanding ground. Measuring on an existing aerial, the distance of that height from the presumed location of the fort is, in fact, approximately 525 yards. This is a little less than the accepted norm of siting a fort at least 600 yards distant from a position of commanding ground. It does seem that the church had a strong natural defense, being on a height of land at the junction point of several roads.

The description of the fortifications denotes that Fort Setauket had a perpendicular picket on top of its parapet walls similar to that described at Fort Slongo. As previously mentioned, this palisade may have been merely a palisade in the ditch or it could have been an actual palisade on top of the embankment. This could have been a unique element not typical of other period redoubts. It could have possibly developed as a vernacular particular to the region.

10

FORT ST. GEORGE

SHIRLEY, NEW YORK

*T*he fort at the Manor of St. George on the south shore of Long Island was constructed by the British in the later years of the Revolution. After the British left Newport, Rhode Island, in 1779, some of the Loyalist refugees settled at the Manor of St. George in Mastic in September 1780. Under the orders of Sir Henry Clinton, their commander, Captain Thomas Hazard, established a post at the location, and it became known as Fort St. George. The force was then known as Thomas Hazard's Corps of Refugees.[110]

On the American side, Benjamin Tallmadge did his own surveillance of the fort in 1780. He recalled it in his later memoirs as follows:

> *A triangular inclosure of several acres of ground at two angles of which was a strong barricade house, and at the third, a fort, with a deep ditch and wall encircled by an abatis of sharpened pickets projecting at an angle of 45 degrees. The fort and houses were entirely connected by a strong stockade, quite high, and every post sharpened and fastened to each other by a transverse rail strongly bolted to each. There were embrazures for six guns, but as yet only two, and these on the water side, were mounted.[111]*

In the autumn of 1780, Major Benjamin Tallmadge of the Second Light Dragoons was ordered by General Washington to attack and destroy the forage collection point at Coram and then possibly attack Fort St. George if it was safe to do so. On November 21, the major mustered two companies of dismounted dragoons and set off from Connecticut. They landed at the village of Old Man's (today called Mount Sinai) after a five-hour crossing, hauled their boats out of the water and concealed them in the woods, leaving a guard of twenty men with them.[112]

After departing the landing point, the men had moved south five miles when a severe storm hit, and they were forced to retreat back to their boats. They sheltered underneath them at the landing place overnight. It was not until the afternoon of the next day that the weather cleared and they were able to set out again in the evening. The force moved along Pipe Stave Hollow to Swezey Pond and then through what at the time was called Millville for the number of mills in the vicinity: Swezey's Mill, Homan's Mill and, at the end of the Connecticut River farther south along the River Road, Carman's Mill.[113] Today, Carman's River is the name for what was then known as the Connecticut River.

The force moved through the night and halted at 4:00 a.m. two miles from the fort to make ready for the assault. Tallmadge placed two small detachments under the command of subalterns Benajah Strong and Thomas Jackson. The plan was for these two groups to attack each side of the triangular stockade while Tallmadge led the rest of the force against the main gate.[114] The attack was solely to be made with guns unloaded—only using the bayonet.

As Tallmadge's section approached, a Loyalist picket in advance of the fort heard their movements and gave the alarm and fired into the darkness. A sergeant beside Tallmadge lunged forward and successfully bayoneted the sentry. The Pioneers (a soldier who performs construction tasks) axed through the gate, making quick access for Tallmadge's force. They headed straight across the *grande parade* (the center of the triangle) and attacked the main fort to the west. They left a platoon at the gate to prevent the enemy from escaping. Tallmadge and his men took the main British fort in ten minutes.[115]

The two other detachments had come through the stockade, and each surrounded the houses at the corners of the triangle. Captives were gathered at the center of the fort, and one officer from each of the detachments mounted the ramparts. From three points, they yelled the watchword: "Washington and Glory." A volley erupted from one of the larger corner houses. Tallmadge ordered his men to load and fire back, and he led his men to storm the house. They axed the barricaded door and forced their way in—fighting hand to hand and throwing the defenders out the second-floor windows.[116] At the same time, another emergency presented itself. The ships at the waterside dock near the fort were preparing to set sail with their

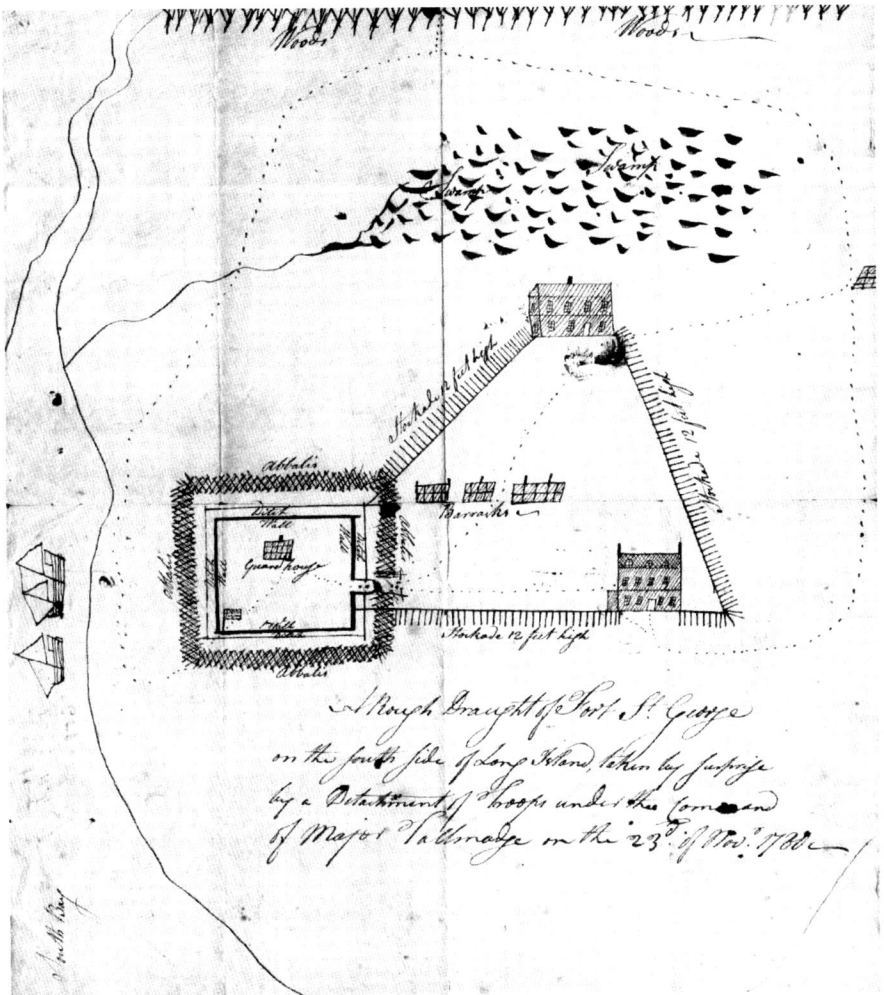

A rough draft of Fort St. George on the south side of Long Island, 1780. Drawing by a Rebel informant, possibly William Booth, showing details of the position. *Courtesy of the Connecticut Historical Society.*

cargo and survivors. The Americans quickly ran out the fort's guns and shut down the threat of their escape. The ships carried valuable supplies and were burned and sunk after their surrender.[117]

After the fighting had stopped, the fortifications and buildings were set on fire and the prisoners were taken. Pinioned in sets of two, they were forced to carry captured goods on their shoulders back to the north side of the island. As the force and prisoners were en route, a small party of ten to twelve men was selected and mounted on horses to make an attack on and destroy the foraging point in Coram. The small force attacked and soon overran the guard and was able to burn the three hundred tons of hay and cornstalks located there. The troops then resumed their march north to the embarkation point. They were in their boats and heading across the sound by 4:00 p.m. on the same day of the attack. They had not lost a man in the battle and had suffered only one wounded. The enemy had seven killed and wounded. Prisoners taken were one lieutenant colonel, the commandant, one lieutenant, one surgeon and fifty rank and file.[118]

A map recorded as "A Rough Draught of Fort St. George on the South Side of Long Island, 1780"—believed to be from a Rebel informant named William Booth—shows a clear plan of the works at the position in 1780. Some of the more interesting notations on this map label the stockade as being twelve feet high between the triangulated corner buildings and the corner fort. This corner fort had all the typical characteristics of a square redoubt of the period. It had a typical redoubt embankment wall, a ditch, an abbatis and a central guardhouse.

Interestingly, this square redoubt's dimensions have been preserved in a form discernable in our present day. The exact dimensional layout of the ditch surrounding this redoubt has survived as a marking in the grass

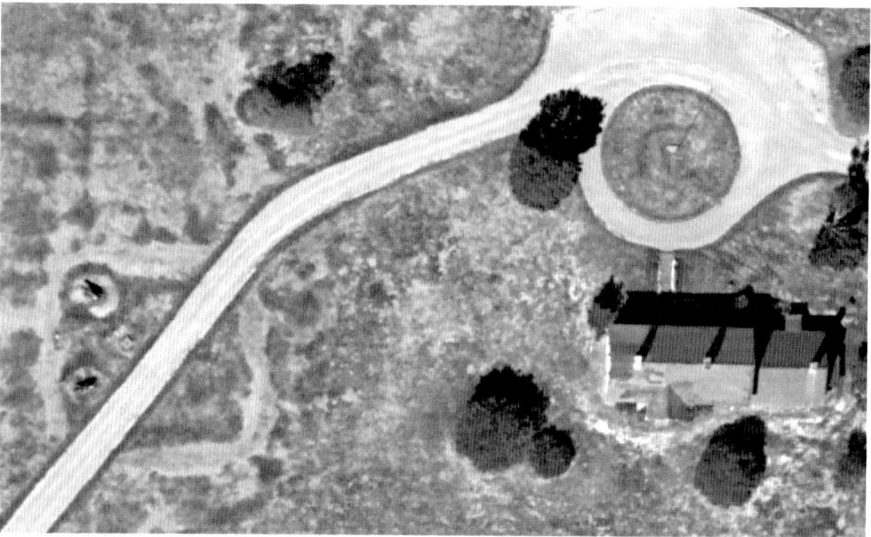

A modern aerial photo showing the burnt grass markings of the former redoubt square ditch clearly seen in the bottom left of the photo. The existing manor house is to the right, Shirley, New York. *Google Maps.*

Panorama view of the manor grounds today looking east and showing the position of the square redoubt. This photo shows how large the triangular picket works were in 1780, Shirley, New York. *Photo by the author.*

caused by a drought that affected the region in 1957. The drought seared the lawns of the site, and later rains partly restored the grass, but a portion of it remained brown, revealing outlines of the trenching of the ditch. Archaeologists confirmed that grass grows thin or discolored where topsoil has been disturbed even after centuries have passed.[119]

Through an analysis by this author of the site and a study of the Booth map, there are interesting findings regarding the layout and dimensions of the fort. The Booth map of the period notes that the redoubt was 90 feet square. The dimensions recorded at the site based on the existing discolored grass markings are approximately 85 feet by 85 feet. An analysis of the rest of the site and its dimensions leads to the conclusion that the map is somewhat accurate in its size and form from the southwest redoubt to the existing manor house and the presumed location of the former northern structure. This would be the triangulated enclosure of the original picketed stockade. By pacing out the dimensions, the longest diagonal sections of the walls were approximately 200 to 250 feet in length—making the fort's overall size vast. This analysis, however, cannot be verified without actual archaeological evidence being studied at the site.

It is interesting to note that in the later years of the war, Sir Henry Clinton, commander of the British army in America, was very critical of the existing forts in use by the Crown forces in the colonies. In March 1779, he wrote:

The very precarious Situation of our Posts in America demands the most serious attention.

It is a maxim in Fortification I believe indisputed, that a work, each exterior side of which is less than 200 yards in length, is incapable of any serious defence: and altho such a Fort to be fully Garrisoned would require a greater number of men than a smaller one; yet with the Garrison necessary for the Latter the Larger work would make a better resistance from the extent of its lines of Defence, from the size of its flanks and from having more room within to take the proper precautions against the effect of shells.—Indeed a work much less cannot be flanked effectively, inconsequently cannot be defended: for redoubts however large and well finished (and even Star-works which have the Show of Flanks without the reality) are of themselves indefensible, and always suppose an army behind them by way of Curtain.[120]

This observation shows the intelligence of the British high command in the latter years of the war regarding advancements in fortifications. It reinforces the uncertainty of the command as well in maintaining the army's defense. Further knowledge and new methods for fortification making needed to be explored. As Clinton's supports a larger fort size, it can only be assumed that the small forts on Long Island at the time fell in with his dislike of all the British posts in America. This may partly explain why some of the forts on Long Island built in the latter years of the war were of such a larger size. Fort St. George may be the largest, employing expanses of curtain walls between structures to support its flanks.

Also of interest in the analysis is that the small, self-contained redoubt at the southwest corner has all of the similar characteristics to other fieldworks of the time and is consistent with other redoubts of the Long Island area. The Booth map shows the parapet wall, a ditch, a sally port, a central blockhouse and a surrounding abbatis. All these features are characteristic of other posts in this book. As mentioned earlier, the fort, however, is unique in its expanse of stockade beyond the redoubt.

One of the more atypical recordings of the fort was the mentioning of the abbatis being a series of sharpened stakes set at a forty-five-degree angle. Although this type of fraizing was typical of battlefield works, it was more commonly used for defending a position from a cavalry attack. The Booth map also shows similar graphical representations for the abbatis to other period maps. In all probability, the abbatis here was the same—made of cut tree canopies that were laid down and positioned so that their branches pointed out and toward a possible attacking force.

Today, the site of the remains of Fort St. George has been thankfully preserved as a park. The park and grounds were acquired by the Town of

Brookhaven in 1974. There was a chance that the site would be developed and the remains destroyed, but it became parkland. The site today comprises a large clearing of space exhibiting a spectacular view of the bay and water beyond. The manor house that was rebuilt after the period of the fort is preserved as well and has a small family cemetery. The cemetery marks the resting places of many of the former inhabitants of the manor.

The site of the fort today still displays many defensive characteristics that lend support to the original siting of the fort within the local geography. The land on which the fort existed is remote from any sort of major road even unto this day. It is flanked by a swampland to its north, a long wooded tract to its east and a waterfront to its south and west.

Although the existing manor house at the park was built after the earlier house was destroyed, it remains an impressive example of an eighteenth-century manor house. The Town of Brookhaven has also established a Benjamin Tallmadge Historic Trail, which marks a walking tour of the route of the attack force all the way from Cedar Beach at Mount Sinai Harbor to the manor grounds. Some of the more interesting sites on the route are the location of the supply depot in Coram, New York, and the position of several historic mills that lined the trail. The mills were originally located along the banks of several small glacial lakes in the island's center. Today, most of the lakes are the pathway of today's Carman's River. One of the original mill buildings—Carman's Mill in South Haven—survived into the late twentieth century. It was built in 1740–45 and survived until 1957, when it was torn down to make way for the Sunrise Highway along the southern shore of Long Island.

11

FORT AT CANOE PLACE

HAMPTON BAYS, NEW YORK

*a*t a location farther east of the Manor of St. George was another
British fort that guarded a pass near the present site of the Shinnecock
Canal. At the time of the Revolutionary War, there was no water passage
between the northern Peconic Bay and the southern Shinnecock Bay. There
was an isthmus of land that connected the present Hampton Bays area to
the village of Southampton farther to the east. This area became known as
the Canoe Place, as it was a popular spot for the Native Americans to launch
their canoes into the Shinnecock Bay.[121]

The main road east to Southampton that passed this point had an estate
adjacent to it with a residence owned by Jeremiah Culver. The house was
built sometime between 1635 and 1640 and was redesigned in 1750 to
become an inn for travelers on the main road.[122] During the Revolutionary
War, it housed British army officers, who also set up the inn as a headquarters
for their use.[123] This house was to become known as the Canoe Place Inn.
On a height of ground behind the inn, the British also built another fort.
This has become known as the Fort at Canoe Place.

There is an existing period map believed to have been drawn by John
André of the fort and redoubt that was proposed to be built on the height.
The map is believed to be from the years 1779–80. André was traveling in
the area with Sir Henry Clinton around this time and may have drawn the
plan to aid in its determination and establishment by the accompanying
commander. There are very limited records about the history of the
fortification at the time, and it seems that it was never attacked or saw any

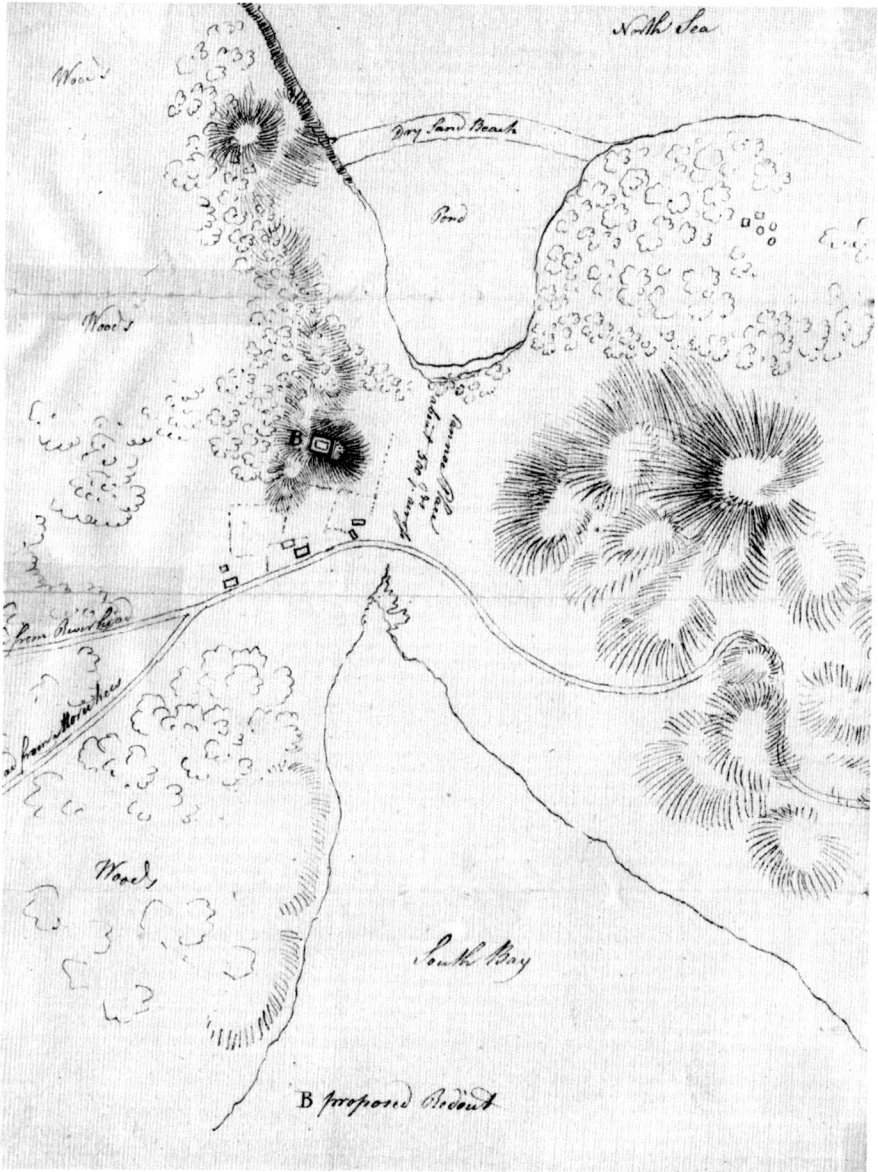

Proposed redoubt at Canoe Place. Believed to be a drawing by John André. The map shows the strategic merits of the fort site. *Courtesy of the William L. Clements Library, the University of Michigan, Ann Arbor, Michigan.*

action. Early historical markers near the site are recorded to have marked the works as of British origin. An author of a 1960 article in the *Long Island Forum* mentions the story of a local resident who claimed that the works were built by the American forces. The story goes that after the British abandoned Boston there was great alarm by the locals and they built the fortifications to prevent a possible march up Long Island by the British to make a rear-guard action against New York City.[124]

Caleb Brewster recorded the following in a surveillance letter to Benjamin Tallmadge in 1779:

> *Dear Sir. I have returned from the Island this day. Genl. Erskine remains yet at Southampton. He has reinforced to the number of 2500. They have three redoubts at South and East Hampton and are heaving up works at Canoe Place at a narrow pass before you get into South Hampton.*[125]

Archibald Robertson of the Royal Engineers wrote in his diary on January 31, 1779, "This Day we Began 4 Redoubts at Southampton. One at the Canoe Place having been begun some time before and 2 Companys of Light Infantry sent there on Detachment."[126]

These two period accounts confirm that the works were, in fact, British and that light infantry units were part of the garrison detachment.

The period map shows that the redoubt was positioned at the optimal point of defense for the area. The isthmus of land and position of the proposed redoubt clearly dominated the passage of the road, the narrow pass of land and the north and south bays.

Luckily, due to the period map and the late residential development of the area, we are able to understand a little more about the fort at the Canoe Place in lieu of any true verifiable information. The earthwork ruins of the fort were photographed and noted as late as 1940, and it seems that they existed even many more years beyond this date. A description of the earthworks from the 1940

Illustration of a British Light Infantryman, 1779. *Courtesy of K/S Historical Publications and Imrie/Risley Miniatures.*

Vintage photo labeled British earthworks. On Peconic Bay are remains of a well-preserved British fort that controlled eastern Long Island during the American Revolution, November 1940. *Courtesy of the East Hampton Library, Long Island Collection.*

vintage photo at that time described the ruins as "a well preserved British Fort." The photo depicts ruined mounds grown over with sod. The site appears to be heavily wooded, and the description noted a wooded path from the main road up to the ruins.

The redoubt appears to be rectangular in plan in the early John André map. An aerial of the site in 1954 shows the outline of a rectangle at the highest point of elevation similar to that noted on the period map. The measured dimensions of the rectangular shape on the aerial photo are approximately ninety by fifty feet. If the markings in the aerial photo are, in fact, the ruins, then the remains of the fort were preserved into the late twentieth century. There appears to be little information about the fort's ruins into our modern day, and a study of the site via aerial photos shows that the area became developed as homes in the late 1980s to mid-1990s. Today, the site can be mapped to the backyards of two adjoining lots. The land is still greatly elevated and shows the defensive significance of this position. Its position today in a cleared state would overlook the whole region to the east and to the west and far out on the waterways to the north and south.

There is an interesting story recorded by Clara Lyons of an incident that took place at the Canoe Place Inn between one of her ancestors and a British commander who was present at the time:

> *Lord Erskine and his men were quartered at the old Inn and an officer waxing bold and saucy threw something at my grandmother at which her husband promptly knocked the man down. Rising, the officer drew his sword and was about to cut my ancestor down when Lord Erskine commanded him to sheath his weapon, saying, "He served you right."*[127]

Lord Erskine became much esteemed on the East End for his good will toward its citizens. Ultimately, it cost him his removal. The original inn building from the time of the Revolution caught fire and burned in 1921. No remains of this original British meeting place exist today.

THE OLD FORT

SOUTHAMPTON, NEW YORK

*S*ix miles to the east of the Canoe Place was the village of Southampton. During the occupation, Southampton had become the headquarters of the British forces in the Eastern District of Long Island. Its development as an important post on the east of Long Island seems to have taken place in the winter of 1778–79. Its commander was General Sir William Erskine, who also commanded forces in Oyster Bay, Jericho and Huntington at different times during the war. He may also have been responsible for the construction of the fortifications at Jericho and Huntington. He is recorded as being the builder of the fortifications on the west side of the village of Southampton in 1778–79:

> *Under the direction of General Erskine, three forts were constructed upon the high ground on West Street, and in the ditches outside the earthworks were thrown masses of cut hedge thorn, which made a most efficient barricade. Mr. William S. Pelletreau was informed many years ago, by an aged man who had been impressed to assist in the work, that the inhabitants were compelled to cut down the thorn hedges for this purpose, and use their oxen and carts in conveying them to the places where needed, and there fill them into the ditches in front of the works.*[128]

In 1778 and 1779, an increase in the number of troops in the area was largely due to the fact that the French alliance with the American army had been signed in February 1779, and a large French fleet was anchored east

Portrait of Sir William Erskine, First Baronet, by Samuel William Reynolds, after Richard Cosway mezzotint, early nineteenth century. *Courtesy of the National Portrait Gallery, London, U.K.*

of Long Island in Newport, Rhode Island.[129] In February 1779, fourteen companies of light infantry, or 700 men, were quartered in Southampton. By March 5, 1779, when General Clinton paid a visit to the village, the number of troops quartered in the village had amassed to 2,500 men. By the end of the month, that number had grown to 4,000. The troops recorded stationed at Southampton were the Seventeenth Regiment of Dragoons, which was a light cavalry unit; the British Legion; and troops of the British Grenadiers and Light Infantry.[130]

The headquarters of General Erskine was in the Pelletreau residence, which was an older house on Main Street. The house no longer exists, but its location is noted on early village maps. Part of the house was used for commissary purposes. The people of the village had fond memories of General Erskine. He would ride his horse to the edge of woods and hills and admire the sea and landscape. He called the area "the garden spot of America."[131] He was very sensitive to the local inhabitants. During his requisitions for supplies, he worked with the locals to be fair, balancing what was available for his use and their own and paying reasonable prices for supplies.[132] This was in the midst of what seems to be a shortage of provisions. A letter from Sir Henry Clinton in 1779 describes the conditions he observed at Southampton: "I much beg leave to say that the troops at Southampton are in the greatest distress for the want of provisions and oats."[133] The size of the forces in Southampton in 1779 stress the village's importance as an eastern base on Long Island.

There is very little written or mapped information on the village of Southampton during the time of the Revolutionary War. In trying to understand the layout of the British forces in the village it is necessary to speculate on the dispositions of possible troops encamped and positions of fortifications. This speculation has become a daunting search for widely dispersed facts and histories.

Pelletreau's mention of three forts west of the village seems to be out of the ordinary for the positioning of fortifications, as most occupied towns had one predominate fortified height. Archibald Robertson of the Royal Engineers also wrote in his diary that they "began construction of 4 redoubts in Southampton in 1779."[134] It is likely that one of these fortifications was the redoubt at the Canoe Place. Although there is precedent for more than one fort at Southampton, such as those at Huntington village, the recordings may have been misinterpreted to mean all the forts that existed in the region. The three forts mentioned by Pelletreau could potentially have been misconstrued as the fort at the Canoe Place, a single redoubt at Southampton and the redoubt at Sag Harbor.

Many regional histories of the town of Southampton note earthworks of the British forces that survived west of Windmill Lane in the village until the early twentieth century. In James Truslow Adam's book *History of the Town of Southampton* is a vintage photo of what the ruins looked like in 1918. The location of these ruins was noted as being a few hundred feet northwest of the Union School building.[135] The Union School building was built in 1890—housing both elementary and high school students—and situated on the present location of the Lola Prentice dog park. There was an older one- to two-room school just north of this that was built in 1857. The Union School building was demolished in 1932.[136]

In the old records of the town of Southampton, a deed for a lot directly to the north of the Union School mentions the ruins of the fort and a windmill that was present on the site at the time: "On the south-east corner of this lot was an old fort built during the Revolution. The windmill stood on the site of the fort. The lot was left to Robert R. Rhodes and his sister Frances Rhodes who sold it to Philanda Payne."[137] Philanda Payne's lot was shown on early maps but was probably much larger when the records were written and most likely extended to the edge of the Union School yard.

In 1932, Lizbeth Halsey White wrote about the ruins of the fort in the *Southampton Press* in the aftermath of the New York State Historical Association conference that was held in Southampton. "The old Fort cast up by the British on the hill back of the colored church was removed only two years ago to make way for a new street which will open up for settlement many choice building sites in a newer Southampton."[138] The church White mentions is the present Sons of Gideon Lodge building at 209 Windmill Lane. The lodge was formerly the Bethel Presbyterian Church, where whites, African Americans and Native Americans gathered for service.[139]

Lizbeth White mentions also in other texts that a new road going west from Bowden Square passed over the site of the old fort.[140] A study by this author of a 1930 aerial of the area is missing White Street. A similar aerial of 1938 shows White Street in its present configuration. The road White mentions can only be presumed to be this street. The only cleared areas visible in the 1930 aerial where a ruin could exist are directly to the south of the path of the future White Street at the end of a small right-of-way road. This right-of-way still exists today and passes by the Gideon Lodge structure, which faces Windmill Lane. This right-of-way is presently very steep, and its elevation plateaus closer to the terminus of the road at the west. This plateau of land is now in the side yards of two newer homes. This location is most likely the former site of the British ruins noted by Adams and White.

Pelletreau also mentions the ruins of a fort on the large farm of George H. White.[141] It is unclear if this ruin is yet another earthwork or the aforementioned site near White Street. George White had an extensive farm

Right: View up the hill today at the right-of-way lane toward the possible location of the former British redoubt, Southampton, New York. *Photo by the author.*

Below: Vintage photo of British earthworks, Southampton. From *A History of Southampton* by James Truslow Adams. *Courtesy of the East Hampton Library, Long Island Collection.*

111

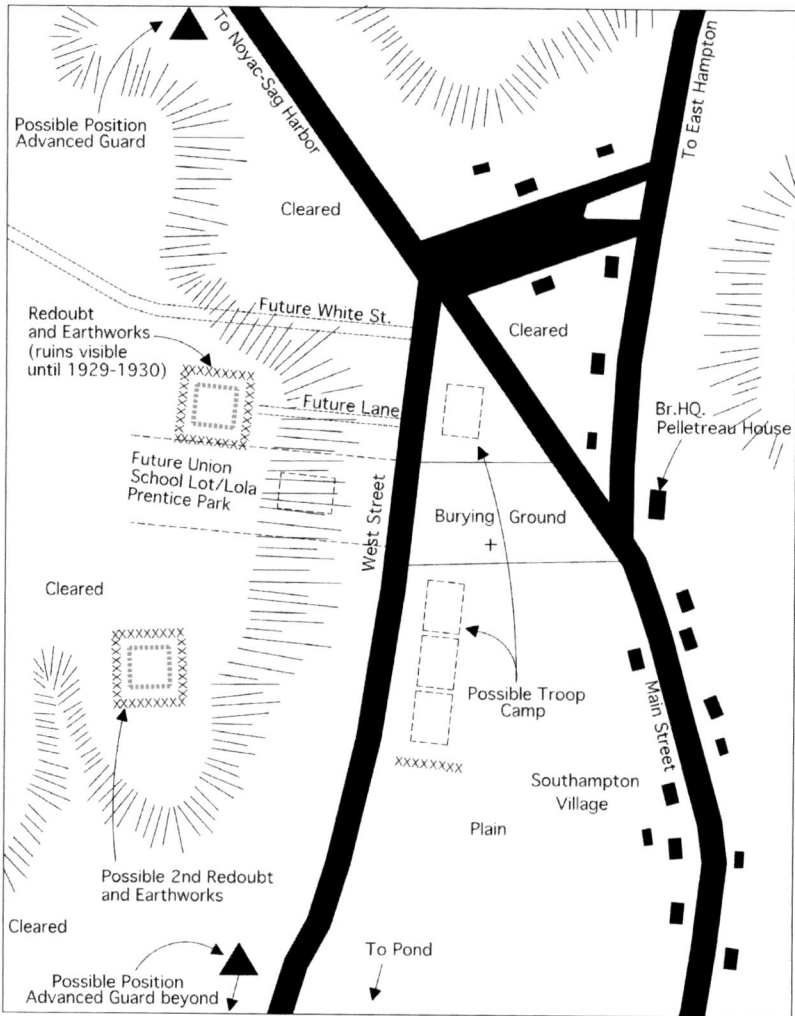

Conjectural map of Southampton village in the Revolutionary War period, 1779.
Map by the author.

to the west of the site and also a strip of land to the south of the Union School lot. This information opens up the possibility that there was, in fact, another fort in the area west of Windmill Lane.

This author has developed a conjectural plan for Southampton during the Revolutionary War period and in the year 1779 reflecting the height of

Vintage postcard of the Old Fort replica that existed at Lola Prentice Park in the village of Southampton in the 1970s. *Courtesy of the Southampton Historical Museum and the Village Historian.*

the occupying forces in the village. The map shows the British headquarters at the location of the old Pelletreau house to the east of the main road. The map also shows the speculated fort location to the west of Windmill Lane (formerly West Street). Both the headquarters house and the fort are along a somewhat linear line parallel with the east–west burying ground plot. The space between the headquarters and the fort also forms a natural valley of flat land. Due to the levelness and location adjacent to Lake Agawan to the south, this could have possibly been the location of troop encampments. The convenience of being surrounded by defenses and the command point and access to nearby water for troop hygiene and use makes it a strong possibility. The fort recorded near the present White Street would most likely have been a typical redoubt of common regular dimensions.

The map also exhibits the possibility that a fort was located south of the White Street position, about a few hundred yards directly south. A possible redoubt position could have existed here on the height of land to the west of Windmill Lane. This fortification may have been located on the grounds of the George White property directly to the south. This speculation seems to coalesce with the natural topography of the general area. The ground is still high but forms a height defendable from the east and west, as the position forms a shallow precipice and would have potentially aided in surveillance of the roadway approach from the west along Hill Street.

The village of Southampton has little record from the period of the American Revolution, but it has been able to maintain some acknowledgement of its spirit during the years of the British occupation. In the years leading up to the 1976 bicentennial, funds were raised to build a redoubt replica on the present height of land at the Lola Prentice Park. A vintage postcard shows the redoubt on the crest of the site. Although the replica lacks accuracy in its representation, it does confirm that there was great local interest and a desire to educate people about the Revolutionary War. This replica was demolished years later like its predecessor. The simple fact that it even existed can be remembered as a spirited approach to historical insight and preservation in the twentieth century.

FORT SAG HARBOR

SAG HARBOR, NEW YORK

*T*he most easterly fort of the British forces recorded was the fort in Sag Harbor. After the fall of Long Island in 1776, the British set up a strong garrison and naval blockade in the Sag Harbor area to prevent supplies from being sent to the American army. A large quantity of supplies and materials had been collected and stored in the town during the early part of the war. On the shore of the harbor in 1776 were two windmills and an old wharf. In 1770, a newer wharf was built and named the Long Wharf. Near the wharf were shipyards that built vessels for local trade use. Sag Harbor had already become an important port for shipping and seafaring trade on the east end.[142]

With the British occupation of the east end, officers were quartered in the house and tavern of James Howell on Main Street, which is the site of the present-day American Hotel. The tavern had a good view of the vessels anchored in the harbor. Troop barracks were set up on Madison Street near Sage Street.[143] The fort was located atop of the Burying Yard Hill and was described as being "a breastwork, enlarged and strengthened by palisades."[144] Records of the battle in 1777 confirm that there were about sixty troops that garrisoned the fort.

In 1777, General Parsons—a commander of the American forces in Connecticut—devised a plan to attack and destroy the supply base at Sag Harbor. This plan was partly planned in retaliation for the burning of Danbury and Ridgefield in Connecticut by British forces led by General Tryon. Parsons discussed the plans with Lieutenant Colonel Jonathan Meigs,

Vintage photo of the outpost captured by Colonel Meigs in the Revolution. The outpost/ hospital was on the Brick Kiln Road. From *A History of Southampton* by James Truslow Adams. *Courtesy of the East Hampton Library, Long Island Collection.*

who was a veteran of the Battle of Bunker Hill and the attack on Quebec with General Arnold. He had been a prisoner of war in Quebec for a year before he was released.[145]

A force of 234 men in thirteen whaleboats embarked from New Haven on May 21, 1777, for the attack of Sag Harbor. The force then went to Guildford, Connecticut, and had to delay the crossing to Long Island until the twenty-third due to the roughness of the sound. Meigs left Guildford in the afternoon of the twenty-third with 170 men and a convoy of two armed sloops and arrived at Southold, Long Island, in the early evening. The whaleboats were transported over the north fork and then the force reembarked on the south shore for the crossing to Sag Harbor.[146] At about midnight, the attack force landed roughly four miles west of the village near the present junction of Noyac Road and Noyac–Long Beach Road.

The force then headed inland to attack an advanced British outpost located two miles from the village along the Brick Kiln Road. Silas Edwards owned a house there that had become an occupied post on this western approach to town. It doubled as a troop hospital for the British forces.[147] The Brick Kiln Road area was already populous by this time, which may have stressed the need for the post there.[148] Two guards were captured at this position

116

and forced to lead the attacking detachment to the British headquarters on Main Street within the village. At the Howell Tavern on Main Street, they captured the commanding officer, Captain James Raymond.[149]

The fort on the brow of the hill at the burying ground was then attacked, and a small skirmish took place. Some histories mention that the fort was taken at bayonet point only. It is difficult to prove this, and there seems to be no evidence that this was the case. The Americans took the position; six of the defenders were killed, and fifty-three were captured.[150]

The American forces then proceeded to the Long Wharf to try to secure the area. A British alarm shot was fired, and an armed twelve-gun schooner started an artillery barrage of the attacking assailants at the wharf. In the end, the American raiders were successful in setting fire to twelve British brigs and sloops that were anchored in the bay. Ninety British sailors were also captured along with large quantities of hay, rum, grain and military and naval supplies. The successful attacking force marched back to its boats with the prisoners. They were back on the Connecticut mainland within twenty-five hours of their initial departure.[151]

The fort's history after 1777 is not well documented. It appears that the British maintained a presence here and in nearby Southampton, Bridgehampton and East Hampton throughout the later years of the war. Records show that part of Delancey's First Battalion resided at Sag Harbor during the 1777 attack.[152] Activities of the British Legion on the east end also attest to its presence at Sag Harbor during the war years. Some of the Legion are recorded as being quartered there in January 1779.[153] Under Major Cochrane, the Legion was also present in Bridgehampton around the same time.[154] The troops may have been only the infantry component of the Legion. The other regiments that were quartered in Southampton were probably also posted in Sag Harbor at different times.

In 1902, monuments were established at the site of the British fort at the burying ground and at the site of the British outpost on the Brick Kiln Road. The site along Brick Kiln Road had become known as the old Polly Payne place.[155] A photo still exists of the old structure that is reputed to have survived of the Brick Kiln outpost building from the time of the Revolution. Due to the relative year of the photo, it seems that the structure existed into the early years of the twentieth century.

The history of the old burying ground at the corner of Union and Madison Streets in Sag Harbor attests to the concerted preservation efforts of local citizens of the time. Historical documents record that the Old Burying Ground was in use by 1770. In these early times, the site was enclosed by a picket fence, and the more southern areas of the burying plot had to be cleared as the cemetery increased in size.[156] At some point in the early nineteenth century, a partial stone wall capped with granite had replaced the earlier picket fence. Part of the wall was jeopardized during the later grading of Madison Street.

In 1859, a local group of citizens held a meeting, and a committee was formed to investigate possible repairs in the Old Burying Ground:

> *They reported that the place was in a deplorable condition and "herds of cattle and troops of unruly boys roamed its grounds, descecrating the ashes of the dead." The stone wall on the Madison Street side was rapidly deteriorating and they were afraid that with the Spring rains, it might collapse and take with it the remains of those buried along the west side. The front row of burials were only two feet from the wall, and in 1860 a decision was made to remove at least fifty and take them to Oakland Cemetery for re-burial. Before the job was over and the wall removed in 1863, the remains of one hundred and thirty-nine individuals were removed.*[157]

With the stone wall removed in 1863, a picket fence was again placed around the cemetery in 1880. The Ladies Village Improvement Society, formed in 1887, donated funds and built the existing iron fencing along

Present view of the embankment of the Old Burying Ground along Madison Street showing the iron fencing from the 1880s, Sag Harbor, New York. *Photo by the author.*

View of the height and flat area above the ridge at the Old Burying Ground today. The area of sunlight in this photo is marking roughly the flat area and assumed position of the former British fort, Sag Harbor, New York. *Photo by the author.*

Madison and Latham Streets. In 1997, a Committee for the Old Burying Ground was set up and a thorough inventory made of the 334 stones in the cemetery.[158]

In 1999, an archaeological dig was carried out on the site with the hopes of unearthing artifacts from the fort. There were some traces of eighteenth- and nineteenth-century habitation, but there weren't any significant discoveries unearthed to confirm this in the random test holes that were made on the site.[159]

This author has done a thorough analysis of the Old Burying Ground site. The crest of the cemetery still preserves a definite ridge at its high point, and this position can still be seen as somewhat of a flat at the existing burying ground plot. The flat area as paced out by the author measures approximately fifty by fifty-five feet square. In the center of the flat area is a depressed area approximately fourteen feet square. This flat is similar to the ruins documented at the Fort Slongo site and suggest that a similar central blockhouse or guardhouse could have existed here at the time.

In all probability, the fort at Sag Harbor was a typical British redoubt of the time in the region. Its overall measurement of fifty feet square attains to the records of other sites on Long Island. The fort probably had the typical ditch and parapet along with the noted palisading of the ditch. It may also have had the aforementioned guardhouse or blockhouse in its center, similar to other works of the period on Long Island.

CONCLUSION

*T*he forts built by the British and Loyalist forces on Long Island two centuries ago today give us a rich collection of historic stories and memories that can be passed down to future generations. There is no doubt that the American Revolution years on Long Island were harsh times for its inhabitants, but it was also a liberating time of dashing acts of courage and unconditional patriotism.

There are some interesting observations that can be considered after viewing and thinking about the British forts as a whole. The forts that were established from Jericho in the west all the way to Setauket in the east could really be thought of as a network of combined positions that fronted and defended against attack from the Long Island Sound and Connecticut to the north. They also acted together as waypoints in a great network of foraging and supply transfer posts. Fort Franklin at Lloyd's Neck assumed the position of headquarters for the British in the region. It was also the largest and most protected of the positions. The southern shore forts were located more toward the east and functioned as transfer points from the southern side of Long Island. Together, these posts created a defended front against enemy attack from the eastern New England colonies. It appears that Southampton acted as the British headquarters for the eastern region of Long Island.

Another observation is that the forts and the establishment of more than one fort per village took place in the areas where there were a greater quantity of town sites and thus a greater combined inhabitant population. Revolutionary War maps of the period clearly show that the northern shore of Long Island had the greatest number of towns—many more than the southern shore area. It makes sense that the areas of greater population provided more supplies and made available more local men for labor forces that were needed by the British. There are several references to locals being pressed into labor to build forts and dig wells for the British army. The forts thus were situated around the more valuable areas of the island possessed of greater resources and manpower. Security of supply lines to these posts also seemed to be most critical.

As much as the writings and analysis of the fort sites demonstrate the similarities between many of the forts, there were also differences as well—products of their particular contexts. As Lewis Lochee affirmed, "A fort's form may be determined by the spot of ground on which it is raised." We can see this theory reflected in the more unique redoubt forms discussed within this book. Some of the fort plans seem to have been strongly influenced by the natural geography of their sites. Also, methods of construction and the use of materials were heavily influenced by the circumstances of each particular position. A lack of wood, which was desperately needed for troop fuel (heating and cooking), and the lack of manpower could have influenced the engineering decision to use earthen walls for most of the fortifications on Long Island. It also could have led army leaders to prefer the reuse and altering of existing buildings in their need for guardhouses, barracks and commissary stores. Local burying grounds were also utilized as sites for forts. Many of the burial grounds of the time were established on high points of land or at positions that were somewhat challenged and difficult to farm or build on. Many times, these sites merely became grazing pastures for local animals, but they had a logistic strength, as they were close to the center of town. As these sites were sometimes the highest point of land in the village and oftentimes cleared, these positions became obvious choices for the establishment of British defensive points. Lastly, most of the posts on Long Island appear to have been established near or adjacent to smaller inland sources of water and ponds. This common characteristic aids greatly in verifying many of their historical locations.

Another interesting observation made in studying the forts is the realization that the cartography of the time was truly an art form. The maps and drawings made by Major Holland show a masterful representation of landscape and clearly demonstrate how a location could be represented as both strategic and defensive within a map. The mapping on the cover of this book by an unknown source shows the layout of the fortifications on

Lloyd's Neck. It captures most of the essential principles that defined the establishment of a fort. Grading, topography, the positioning of works and troops and the representation of points of uniqueness are all noted in the drawing. This drawing served as a means to capture and record a moment in time. In my mind, the work successfully captures the full essence of the art of fortification making.

This book attempts to put together and relate a number of historic sites all located within a similar geographical area and of a similar historical period and cultural heritage. Research can be further deduced from other period records, more analysis and from additional study of existing historical fabric. Many of the sites are located in either public cemeteries, parks or municipal lands and thus allow for ongoing access and research to be carried out on them. Thankfully, due to many of the forts' early institutional positioning, such as in graveyards and churchyards, these sites have been able to survive unto this day without being built over. Some of the sites are on private land, which we hope will be respected and preserved for years to come. Remains of forts that have survived in physical form may at some point become interesting archaeological sites of future and ongoing research.

Preservation in any formal sense of the fort sites has not taken place. There are no registered or recognized historical designations of mostly all these fort sites except for that of Fort Franklin on Lloyd's Neck. At this site, an architect chose to integrate the ruins of the fort into a manor house courtyard and thus preserved some of the fort's historical fabric. At Fort Slongo, the ruins were lucky enough to have survived the construction of a residential neighborhood around them. At Fort St. George, the outlines of the fort's redoubt were naturally preserved by the burning of grass during a severe time of drought. In the village of Southampton, the remains of its British fort were bulldozed in the 1930s to make way for a modern road, but it appears that there was no local press coverage of the event.

Today, there is once again an opportunity and a responsibility to preserve the remains of these historic sites. With this endeavor, we will be able to learn more about our own Revolutionary War history while ensuring that the existing stories of Long Island's early history will also survive for generations to come.

NOTES

Introduction

1. Ross and Pelletreau, *History of Long Island, From Its Earliest Settlement to the Present Time*, vol 2, 201–2.

Chapter 1

2. Lochee, *Elements of Field Fortification*, 1.
3. Muller, *Treatise Containing the Practical Part of Fortification*, 122–28.
4. "Geometry of War: Fortification Plans from 18th Century America," an electronic version of the Great Room exhibit: formerly on display at the William L. Clements Library, October 15, 2012–February 15, 2013, Case 1–8.
5. Lydenberg, *Archibald Robertson Lieutenant-General Royal Engineers, His Diaries and Sketches in America 1762–1780*.
6. "Geometry of War," Case 7.
7. Hart, "Forts on the Frontier—Adapting European Military Engineering to North America," 22.
8. Lochee, *Elements of Field Fortification*, 36–37.
9. Cubbison, "Historic Structures Report: The Redoubts of West Point," 4.
10. Lochee, *Elements of Field Fortification*, 36–37.
11. Hart, "Forts on the Frontier—Adapting European Military Engineering to North America," 21.

12. Pleydell, *Essay on Field Fortification: Intended Principally for the Use of Officers of Infantry, Showing How to Trace Out on the Ground and Construct in the Easiest Manner, All Sorts of Redoubts and Other Field Works*, 14.

13. Pleydell, *Essay on Field Fortification*, 8–9.

14. Lochee, *Elements of Field Fortification*, 8.

15. Ibid., 8, 10–11.

16. Ibid., 16–17, 24–25.

17. Ibid., 21.

18. Cubbison, "Historic Structures Report," 8.

19. Lochee, *Elements of Field Fortification*, 14.

20. "Geometry of War," Case 5.

21. Cubbison, "Historic Structures Report," 8.

22. Lochee, *Elements of Field Fortification*, 119.

23. Ibid., 120–24.

24. Gross, *Duties of an Officer in the Field; and Principally of Light Troops, Whether Cavalry or Infantry*, 22.

25. Ford, *Orderly Book of the Maryland Loyalists Regiment, June 18th, 1778, to October 12th, 1778. Kept by Captain Caleb Jones*, 22–34.

26. *History of Queens County with Illustrations, Portraits & Sketches of Prominent Families and Individuals*, 148.

Chapter 2

27. Onderdonk, *Documents and Letters Intended to Illustrate the Revolutionary Incidents of Queens County: With Connecting Narratives, Explanatory Notes, and Additions*, 206.

28. Ford, *Orderly Book of the Maryland Loyalists Regiment*, 15.

29. "Seth Norton Papers L 82.2.48."

30. Onderdonk, *Documents and Letters Intended to Illustrate the Revolutionary Incidents of Queens County*, 217, 247.

31. "Seth Norton Papers L 82.2.48."

32. Onderdonk, *Documents and Letters Intended to Illustrate the Revolutionary Incidents of Queens County*, 209–10.

33. "To George Washington from Brigadier General Charles Scott, 10 November 1778," (Founders Online, National Archives, last modified December 28, 2016).

34. Onderdonk, *Documents and Letters Intended to Illustrate the Revolutionary Incidents of Queens County: With Connecting Narratives, Explanatory Notes, and Additions. Second Series*, 19.

35. Gross, *Duties of an Officer in the Field*, 22–23.

36. Ibid., 24–26.

37. Ryan, "Fort Nonsense in Jericho," March 28, 1977.

38. "Quitclaim of Rights in Two Home Lots and a Parcel Called the Flat Land, All at Jericho. In Oyster Bay Township, NY: by Mary Townsend, Widow of Doctor James Townsend, Deceased, Late of Said Jericho to John Jackson, of South Hempstead Township, NY., April 7, 1795," East Hampton Public Library, Long Island Collection, East Hampton, New York.

39. Kelly, *Domestic Architecture of Connecticut*, 17.

40. "Rep. No.: L55.16.1 Original, list. List of British Soldiers Quartered at Jericho, 1783," Long Island Studies Institute Collections, Nassau County Museum, Hempstead, New York.

41. Carpenter, *History and Genealogy of the Carpenter Family in America from the Settlement at Providence, R.I. 1637–1901*, 72.

42. Murphy, *Jericho: The History of a Long Island Hamlet*, 75–76.

Chapter 3

43. Van Santvoord, "Colonel Simcoe's Fort," 9.

44. Onderdonk, *Documents and Letters Intended to Illustrate the Revolutionary Incidents of Queens County*, 212–13.

45. Simcoe, *Simcoe's Military Journal. A History of the Operations of a Partisan Corps Called the Queen's Rangers, Commanded by Lieut. Col. J.G. Simcoe, During the War of the American Revolution*, 93–94.

46. Van Santvoord, "Colonel Simcoe's Fort," 9.

47. Onderdonk, *Documents and Letters Intended to Illustrate the Revolutionary Incidents of Queens County*, 213–32.

48. Gara, *Queen's American Rangers*, 177.

49. Van Santvoord, "Colonel Simcoe's Fort," 10.

50 Gross, *Duties of an Officer in the Field*, 22.

Chapter 4

51. Valentine, "Fort Franklin," 163.

52. Onderdonk, *Documents and Letters Intended to Illustrate the Revolutionary Incidents of Queens County*, 223.

53. Ibid., 221.

54. Valentine, "Fort Franklin," 164.

55. Ibid., 164.

56. *Long Islander*, "Lloyds Neck History," May 4, 1923, 15.

57. Samuelsen, "Forts of Huntington," 4.

58. "A Sketch of Lloyd's Neck: Particularly Shewing the Situation of the Redoubt, Encampment of the Troops, with the Ground Adjacent and Position of the Advanc'd Picket's," a map courtesy of the William L. Clements Library, the University of Michigan, Ann Arbor, Michigan.

59. Valentine, "Fort Franklin," 164.

60. Metcalf, "Account of the Battle of Fort Franklin," July 9, 1981.

61. Ibid.

62. Ibid.

63. Ibid.

64. Davidson, "A Loyalist Refugee Camp." *Loyalist Trails* UELAC Newsletter 2009 Archive, 2,009–31, August 2, 2009.

65. McCarthy, "History Is Her Fort," 144.

66. Woolsey, "Lloyd Manor of Queens Village," address delivered at the eleventh annual meeting of the New York Branch of the Colonial Lords of Manors in America, New York, April 27, 1923.

67. McCarthy, "History Is Her Fort," 144.

68. Lochee, *Elements of Field Fortification*, 12.

69. Ibid, 36.

70 *Long Islander*, "Lloyds Neck History," 15.

Chapter 5

71. Metcalf, "Account of the Battle of Fort Franklin."

72. "A Sketch of Lloyd's Neck."

73. Onderdonk, *Documents and Letters Intended to Illustrate the Revolutionary Incidents of Queens County*, 222.

74. "Target Rock Farm (Lloyd Harbor, New York)," http://wikimapia.org/6028944/Target-Rock-Farm.

Chapter 6

75. Reynolds, *Long Island Behind the British Lines during the Revolution*, 20–21.

76. Platt, "Old Times in Huntington," address delivered at the Centennial Celebration at Huntington, Suffolk County, NY, July 1876, 59–61.

77. Street, *Huntington Town Records, Including Babylon, Long Island, New York (1776–1873)*, vol. 3, 83–84.
78. Platt, "Old Times in Huntington," 60.
79. "Old First Presbyterian Church," excerpted and paraphrased from Alfred B. Sforza, *Portrait Of A Small Town II: Huntington, New York* (Huntington, NY: Fore Angels Press, 2001).
80. Lott, "Fort Golgotha," 158.
81. Street, *Huntington Town Records*, 84.

Chapter 7

82. Platt, "Old Times in Huntington," 58.
83. *Long Islander,* "Facts about Hunt's Revolutionary Cem'ry," 22.
84. Ibid, 34.
85. Ibid, 34–35.
86. *Orderly Book of the Three Battalions of Loyalist Commanded by Brigadier-General Oliver De Lancey 1776–1778*, 23.
87. Platt, "Old Times in Huntington," 59.
88. Samuelsen "Forts of Huntington," 2–3.
89. Ibid, 3.
90. Ibid.
91. *Long Islander*, "Fort Hill and How It Was Named," April 29, 1927, 11.
92. *Orderly Book of the Three Battalions of Loyalist Commanded by Brigadier-General Oliver De Lancey 1776–1778*, 27.

Chapter 8

93. Welch, *General Washington's Commando: Benjamin Tallmadge in the Revolutionary War*, 184.
94 Irwin, "Fort Slongo," 151.
95. Ibid.
96. Early plan sketch layout of Fort Slongo and surroundings believed to be drawn by a Patriot spy. Courtesy of the Library of Congress.
97. Irwin, "Fort Slongo," 152.
98. Ibid.
99. Ibid.
100. Ibid.

Chapter 9

101. Strong, "Setauket in the Revolution," 227.
102. Ibid.
103. Ibid.
104. Ibid, 228.
105. "Patriot's Rock," Three Village Community Trust, http://www.threevillagecommunitytrust.org/new-page-3.
106. Lochee, *Elements of Field Fortification*, 102–5.
107. Ibid, 113.
108. Ibid, 114–15.
109. Klein, *Three Village Guidebook*, 58–59.

Chapter 10

110. Allen and Braisted, *The Loyalist Corps: Americans in Service to the King*, 45,46.
111. Tallmadge, *Memoir of Colonel Benjamin Tallmadge, Prepared at the Request of His Children*, 39.
112. Lohse, "Battle of St. George's Manor," 143.
113. Ibid, 144.
114. Ibid, 152.
115. Ibid.
116. Tallmadge, *Memoir of Colonel Benjamin Tallmadge*, 41.
117. Ibid.
118. Ibid, 42.
119. *Manor of St. George, Situated at Smith's Point, near Mastic Beach, Suffolk County, Long Island, New York*, dedication booklet as a public museum and park, 1955.
120. "March 13, 1779," *Henry Clinton papers 1736–1850, March 11, 1779–March 31, 1779*, vol. 54, William L. Clements Library, University of Michigan, Ann Arbor, Michigan

Chapter 11

121. Cooper, "Brief History of the Canoe Place Inn," November 23, 2010.
122. Ibid.
123. Josiah C. Pumpelly, "Historical Sketches of the Hampton Settlements on Long Island," *Americana* VI (January 1911): 230.

124. Raynor, "Earthworks?," 43.
125. Brewster, "Collection of Letters." Series 4, General Correspondence: Caleb Brewster to Benjamin Tallmadge, February 26, 1779 (Library of Congress, American Memory, George Washington Papers, 1741–1799).
126. Lydenberg, *Archibald Robertson Lieutenant-General Royal Engineers*, 188.
127. *Americana* (American Historical Magazine) Vol. VI., 230.

Chapter 12

128. Ross and Pelletreau, *History of Long Island*, 483.
129. O'Sullivan, *East Hampton and the American Revolution*, 48.
130. Ibid., 48–49.
131. Ross and Pelletreau, *History of Long Island*, 484.
132. Ibid.
133. "Islip 25th of March 1779." *Henry Clinton Papers 1736–1850, March 11, 1779–March 31, 1779*, vol. 54, William L. Clements Library, University of Michigan, Ann Arbor, Michigan.
134. Lydenberg, *Archibald Robertson Lieutenant-General Royal Engineers*, 188.
135. Adams, *History of the Town of Southampton (East of Canoe Place)*, 173.
136. Cummings, *Southampton*, 84.
137. Pelletreau and Early, *Sixth Volume of Record of Southampton, L.I., N.Y.*, 229.
138. Halsey, "Historical Association Aftermath-Southampton Press Thursday, October 17, 1932. Written by the Late Mrs. Edward P. White on the Day of Her Death, Tuesday, October 25, 1932." *Notes on the Jesse Halsey History Project*, 2012. http://halseyhelgesontree.blogspot.com/2012/09/historical-association-aftermath.html.
139. Spanburgh, "209 Windmill Lane (Sons of Gideon Lodge)," June 24, 2010.
140. White, "Southampton—Her Records and Her Landmarks," 378.
141. Ross and Pelletreau, *History of Long Island*, 483.

Chapter 13

142. Zaykowski. *Sag Harbor, The Story of an American Beauty*, 58.
143. O'Sullivan, *East Hampton and the American Revolution*, 49.
144. Zaykowski. *Sag Harbor*, 58.
145. Ibid.

146. Ibid.

147. Ibid., 58–59.

148. Sleight, *Sag Harbor in Earlier Days: A Series of Historical Sketches of the Harbor and Hampton Port*, 90.

149. Zaykowski, *Sag Harbor*, 59.

150. Underhill, "Old Burying Ground." Sag Harbor Chamber of Commerce.

151. Zaykowski, *Sag Harbor*, 58.

152. Allen, *The Loyalist Corps*, 33.

153. Robertson, *Archibald Robertson Lieutenant-General Royal Engineers*, 188.

154. Adams, *History of the Town of Southampton*, 172.

155. Meigs, *Record of the Descendants of Vincent Meigs, Who Came from Dorsetshire, England. To America about 1635*, 326.

156. Zaykowski and Members of the Committee for the Old Burying Ground, *Old Burying Ground at Sag Harbor, L.I., N.Y.*, 1.

157. Ibid, 2.

158. Ibid, 2–3.

159. Ibid, 3.

Bibliography

Primary Sources

Brewster, Caleb. "Collection of Letters Including General Correspondence with George Washington, Samuel Culper, Benjamin Tallmadge, David Humphreys, and David Waterbury," 1778–1784. Series 4, General Correspondence: Caleb Brewster to Benjamin Tallmadge, February 26, 1779, Library of Congress, American Memory, George Washington Papers, 1741–1799.

Ford, Paul L., ed. *Orderly Book of the Maryland Loyalists Regiment, June 18th, 1778, to October 12th, 1778. Kept by Captain Caleb Jones.* Brooklyn, NY: Historical Printing Club, 1891.

Gross, Baron. *Duties of an Officer in the Field; and Principally of Light Troops, Whether Cavalry or Infantry.* London: printed for C. Roworth, 1801.

Henry Clinton Papers 1736–1850, March 11, 1779–March 31, 1779. Vol. 54. William L. Clements Library, University of Michigan.

Henry Onderdonk Papers, ARC.045, Box 1 and Folder 4–7. Brooklyn Historical Society.

Howell, George Rogers. *The Early History of Southampton, L.I., New York with Genealogies.* Albany, NY: Weed, Parsons and Company, 1887.

John Graves Simcoe Papers 1774–1824: Correspondence and Documents. William L. Clements Library, University of Michigan.

Johnston, Henry Phelps. *The Campaign of 1776 around New York and Brooklyn.* New York: Da Capo Press, 1878.

Lengel, Edward G., ed. *The Papers of George Washington, Revolutionary War Series*. Vol. 18. Charlottesville: University of Virginia Press, 2008.

Lochee, Lewis. *Elements of Field Fortification*. London: T. Cadell and T. Egerton, 1783.

Long Island Studies Institute Collections, Nassau County Museum, Rep. No.: L55.16.1 Original, list. List of British soldiers quartered at Jericho, 1783.

Lydenberg, Harry Miller, ed. *Archibald Robertson Lieutenant-General Royal Engineers, His Diaries and Sketches in America 1762–1780*. New York: New York Public Library, 1930.

Muller, John. *A Treatise Containing the Practical Part of Fortification. In Four Parts*. London: printed for A. Millar, 1755.

Onderdonk, Henry Jr. *Documents and Letters Intended to Illustrate the Revolutionary Incidents of Queens County: With Connecting Narratives, Explanatory Notes, and Additions*. New York: Leavitt, Trow and Company, 1846.

———. *Documents and Letters Intended to Illustrate the Revolutionary Incidents of Queens County: With Connecting Narratives, Explanatory Notes, and Additions. Second Series*. Hempstead, NY: Lott Van de Water, 1884.

Orderly Book of the Three Battalions of Loyalists Commanded by Brigadier-General Oliver De Lancey 1776–1778. Baltimore, MD: Genealogical Publishing, 1972.

Pelletreau, William S., and James A. Early. *The Sixth Volume of Record of Southampton, L.I., N.Y. Being Abstracts of Vol.II of Deeds in the Town Clerk's Office with Additional Unrecorded Deeds with Indexes of Names and Localities*. Sag Harbor, NY: John H. Hunt, 1915.

Platt, Henry C. "Old Times in Huntington." Address delivered at the Centennial Celebration at Huntington, Suffolk County, NY, July 1876.

Pleydell, Lieutenant J.C. *An Essay on Field Fortification: Intended Principally for the Use of Officers of Infantry, Showing How to Trace Out on the Ground and Construct in the Easiest Manner, All Sorts of Redoubts and Other Field Works*. London: printed for J. Nourse, Bookseller to His Majesty, 1768.

"Quitclaim of Rights in Two Home Lots and a Parcel Called the Flat Land, All at Jericho. In Oyster Bay Township, NY: by Mary Townsend, Widow of Doctor James Townsend, Deceased, Late of Said Jericho to John Jackson, of South Hempstead Township, NY., April 7, 1795." East Hampton Public Library, Long Island Collection.

Ross, Peter, and William S. Pelletreau. *History of Long Island, From Its Earliest Settlement to the Present Time*. Vol. 2. New York: Lewis Publishing Company, 1905.

"Seth Norton Papers L 82.2.48." Long Island Studies Institute Collections, Nassau County Museum, Hempstead, New York.

Simcoe, Lieutenant Colonel John Graves. *Simcoe's Military Journal. A History of the Operations of a Partisan Corps called The Queen's Rangers, Commanded by Lieut. Col. J.G. Simcoe, During the War of the American Revolution.* New York: Bartlett & Welford, 1844.

"A Sketch of Lloyd's Neck: Particularly Shewing the Situation of the Redoubt, Encampment of the Troops, with the Ground Adjacent and Position of the Advanc'd Picket's." William L. Clements Library, the University of Michigan, Ann Arbor, Michigan.

Stevens, John Austin. *The Magazine of American History with Notes and Queries.* Vol. 8. Edited by Martha J. Lamb. New York: A.S. Barnes, 1882.

Street, Charles R. *Huntington Town Records, Including Babylon, Long Island, New York (1776–1873).* Vol. 3. Huntington, NY: 1887.

Tallmadge, Benjamin. *Memoir of Colonel Benjamin Tallmadge, Prepared at the Request of His Children.* New York: T. Holman, 1858.

Willcox, William Bradford, ed. *The American Rebellion: Sir Henry Clinton's Narrative of His Campaigns, 1775–1782.* New Haven, CT: Yale University Press, 1954.

Secondary Sources

Adams, James Truslow. *History of the Town of Southampton (East of Canoe Place).* Bridgehampton, NY: Hampton Press, 1918.

Allen, Thomas B., and Todd W. Braisted. *The Loyalist Corps: Americans in Service to the King.* Takoma Park, MD: Foxacre Press, 2011.

Braisted, Todd W. *The Online Institute for Loyalist Studies.* Last Modified February 7, 2015. http://www.royalprovincial.com.

Carpenter, Daniel Hoogland. *History and Geneology of the Carpenter Family in America from the Settlement at Providence, R.I. 1637–1901.* Jamaica, NY: Marion Press, 1901.

Chartrand, Rene. *American Loyalist Troops 1775–84.* Oxford: Osprey Publishing Inc., 2008.

Cooper, Laura. "A Brief History of the Canoe Place Inn." *Southampton Press,* November 23, 2010.

Cubbison, Douglas R. "Historic Structures Report. The Redoubts of West Point." West Point, NY: U.S. Military Academy, 2004.

Cummings, Mary. *Southampton, New York.* Charleston, SC: Arcadia Publishing, 1996.

Davidson, Stephen. "A Loyalist Refugee Camp." *Loyalist Trails* (August 2009): 31.

Epstein, Jason, and Elizabeth Barlow. *East Hampton: A History and Guide.* Sag Harbor, NY: Medway Press Inc., 1975.

Furman, George C. *The Manor of St. George, Situated at Smith's Point, near Mastic Beach, Suffolk County, Long Island, New York.* Dedication booklet as a public museum and park, 1955.

Gara, Donald J. *The Queen's American Rangers.* Yardley: Westholme Publishing, 2015.

"The Geometry of War: Fortification Plans from 18th Century America." An electronic version of the Great Room exhibit formerly on display at the William L. Clements Library, October 15, 2012–February 15, 2013.

Halsey, Anne. "Historical Association Aftermath-Southampton Press Thursday, October 17, 1932. Written by the Late Mrs. Edward P. White on the Day of Her Death, Tuesday, October 25, 1932." *Notes on the Jesse Halsey History Project,* 2012. http://halseyhelgesontree.blogspot.com/2012/09/historical-association-aftermath.html

Halsey, William Donaldson. *Sketches from Local History.* Bridgehampton, NY: H. Lee, 1935.

Harris, Brad. *The Battle of Ft. Slongo, Oct. 3ʳᵈ 1781.* Fort Salonga, NY: Fort Salonga Association, 2015.

Hart, James L. "Forts on the Frontier—Adapting European Military Engineering to North America." In *The Archaeology of French and Indian War Frontier Forts,* edited by Lawrence Babits and Stephanie Gandulla, 17–51. Gainesville: University Press of Florida, 2015.

History of Queens County with illustrations, Portraits & Sketches of Prominent Families and Individuals. New York: W.W. Munsell & Company, 1882.

Horton, H.P. "Meigs' Raid on Sag Harbor." *Long Island Forum* 4, no. 7 (1941): 155.

Irwin, C. Russell. "Fort Slongo." *Long Island Forum* 23, no. 7 (1960): 151–52.

Kelly, Frederick J. *The Domestic Architecture of Connecticut.* New York: Dover Publications, Inc., 1952.

Klein, Howard. *Three Village Guidebook: The Setaukets, Old Field and Stony Brook.* Victoria, BC: Trafford Publishing, Three Village Historical Society, 2002.

Lohse, Roland. "The Battle of St. George's Manor." *Long Island Forum* 17, no. 8 (1954): 143–44, 152.

Long Islander (Huntington, NY). "Facts about Hunt's Revolutionary Cem'ry." August 5, 1927.

———. "Fort Hill and How It Was Named." April 29, 1927.

———. "Lloyds Neck History—The Discovery of Skeletons Brings to Light Some Interesting Data." May 4, 1923.

Lott, Ray E. "Fort Golgotha." *Long Island Forum* 24, no. 7 (1961): 157–58, 164.

Luke, Myron H., and Robert W. Venables. *Long Island in the American Revolution.* Albany: New York State American Revolution Bicentennial Commission, 1976.

Luzader, John F. *Fort Stanwix: Construction and Military History.* Fort Washington, MD: Eastern National, 2001.

Magnani, E. "Seth Norton, Tory Forager." *The Freeholder* 2, no. 1 (1997): 5–6, 15.

Mather, Frederic Gregory. *The Refugees of 1776 from Long Island to Connecticut.* Albany, NY: J.B. Lyon Company, Printers, 1913.

May, Robin. *The British Army in North America 1775–83.* Rev. ed. Oxford: Osprey Publishing, 1990.

McCarthy, Molly. "History Is Her Fort." in *Long Island: Our Story 1998.* Hempstead, NY: Newsday Books, 1998, 144.

Meigs, Henry B. *Record of the Descendants of Vincent Meigs, Who Came from Dorsetshire, England. To America about 1635.* Baltimore: J.S. Bridges & Company, 1902.

Metcalf, Reginald H. Jr. "An Account of the Battle of Fort Franklin." *Long Islander,* July 9, 1981.

Murphy, Betsey. *Jericho: The History of a Long Island Hamlet.* Cold Spring Harbor, NY: Rosalie Ink Publications, 2009.

O'Sullivan, Ilse. *East Hampton and the American Revolution.* East Hampton, NY: East Hampton Town Bicentennial Committee, 1976.

Pumpelly, Josiah C. "Historical Sketches of the Hampton Settlements on Long Island." *Americana* VI (January 1911).

Raynor Joseph. "Earthworks?" *Long Island Forum* 23, no. 2 (1960): 43.

Reynolds, John. *Long Island Behind the British Lines during the Revolution.* Setauket, NY: The Society for the Preservation of Long Island Antiquities, 1960.

Roberts, Robert B. *New York's Forts in the Revolution.* London: Fairleigh Dickinson University Press, 1980.

Ryan, Richard. "Fort Nonsense in Jericho." Memo to members and colleagues of former Nassau Museum. March 28, 1977.

Salmon, Stuart. "The Loyalist Regiments of the American Revolutionary War 1775–1783." PhD Dissertation, University of Stirling, UK, 2009.

Samuelsen, S. Gunter. "Forts of Huntington." Report for Huntington Chamber of Commerce, n.d.

Schecter, Barnet. *The Battle for New York, The City at the Heart of the American Revolution.* New York: Walker Publishing, 2002.

Sleight, Harry D. *Sag Harbor in Earlier Days. A Series of Historical Sketches of the Harbor and Hampton Port.* Sag Harbor: Hampton Press, 1930.

Southampton (NY) Times. "The Old Mill Hill Mill." August 24, 1928.

Spanburgh, Sally. "209 Windmill Lane (Sons of Gideon Lodge)." *Southampton Village Review,* June 24, 2010.

Strong, Kate W. "Setauket in the Revolution." *Long Island Forum* 11, no. 12 (1948): 227–28.

Tiedeman, Joseph S. and Eugene R. Fingerhut, eds. *The Other New York: The American Revolution Beyond New York City, 1763–1787.* Albany: State University of New York Press, 2006.

Underhill, Lois Beachy. "Old Burying Ground." Carol's House. http://www.carolshouse.com.

Valentine, Andrus T. "Fort Franklin." *Long Island Forum* 38, no. 9 (1975): 163–66.

Van Santvoord, Peter L. "Colonel Simcoe's Fort." *Long Island Forum* 27, no. 1 (1964): 9–12.

Wardell, Pat. "Early Bergen County Families." Genealogical Society of Bergen Online Database, 2017. http://njgsbc.org/indexes/bergen-county-families.

Welch, Richard F. *General Washington's Commando: Benjamin Tallmadge in the Revolutionary War.* Jefferson, NC: McFarland, 2014.

White, Lizbeth Halsey. "Southampton—Her Records and Her Landmarks." *New York History* 14, no. 4 (1933): 378.

Woolsey, Reverend Melancthon Lloyd. "The Lloyd Manor of Queens Village." Address delivered at the eleventh Annual Meeting of the New York Branch of the Colonial Lords of Manors in America, New York, April 27, 1923.

Zaykowski, Dorothy Ingersoll. *The Old Burying Ground at Sag Harbor, L.I., N.Y.* Berwyn Heights, MD: Heritage Books Inc., 2003.

———. *Sag Harbor, The Story of an American Beauty.* Sag Harbor, NY: Sag Harbor Historical Society, 1991.

INDEX

About the Author

David M. Griffin is a practicing architectural and interior designer based in the New York area and an independent architectural historian and researcher. Professionally trained as an architect in Ottawa, Canada, he has lived and worked in Toronto, Boston and New York City. He has always held a fascination for early history and especially early fortifications of North America. He grew up intrigued by the geometries of British forts in his native province of Ontario, visiting these historic sites whenever possible. Presently, his independent research focuses on colonial-era architecture and structures. Through his professional work and his independent research, he strives for a greater understanding of architectural history and its possible influences on contemporary design. He lives with his family on the north shore of Long Island.